Edited by Hilary Jastram

www.bookmarkpub.com

CHOOSE YOU

FOR THE PEOPLE WHO REFUSE TO DISAPPEAR

CANDICE MITCHELL

Disclaimer/Disclosure

I am not a medical doctor, licensed psychologist, or mental health professional, and nothing in this book should be interpreted as medical, psychological, or therapeutic advice. The content shared here is not intended to diagnose, treat, cure, or prevent any condition, nor should it replace professional care. If you are experiencing mental health challenges or need clinical support, please seek guidance from a qualified professional.

The archetypes, reflections, and frameworks in this book are not based on peer-reviewed research, double-blind studies, or formal scientific trials. There are no control groups, no lab coats, and no grant funding behind them. What *is* behind them is postgraduate study in psychology and organizational leadership, years of work across learning, talent, and change, and hundreds of conversations with people navigating identity, work, ambition, and belonging.

These insights are observational rather than empirical. They emerged through listening, noticing patterns, and connecting themes across real human experiences. The archetypes are not diagnoses or labels. They are lenses, intended to support reflection, self-awareness, and choice.

This book is provided for informational and reflective purposes only. Neither the author nor the publisher shall be held responsible or liable for any financial, emotional, personal, incidental, or consequential outcomes, losses, or damages that may arise from the use or interpretation of the ideas, exercises, or perspectives shared within these pages. Any actions you take as a result of reading this book are your own responsibility.

If something in these pages resonates, you are free to explore it further. If something doesn't, you are equally free to leave it behind. This book offers perspective, not prescription.

And for the record, no scientists, psychologists, or governing bodies of personality assessments were harmed in the making of this book. Please don't report me to them. We're all just trying to understand ourselves a little better.

Additionally, the names and circumstances in this book have been changed to protect identities. Any resemblance to persons living or dead is coincidental.

Dedication

To my dad and mom,

"Because You Loved Me," by Diane Warren

Get in Touch

You're here because you care about people, growth, and work that matters, and you've found your place.

Start at ChooseYouBook.com—the home of *Choose You: For the People Who Refuse to Disappear*.

There, you'll find regularly updated resources, upcoming events, and the application form for speaking engagements or People-team workshops.

Want insights on the go? Check out the ***Development Nerds* podcast** and **YouTube channel**, hosted by Candice Mitchell, for practical tools and honest stories about leading with impact.

Curious where you stand?

Start with the How Invisible Are You at Work? quiz. It's a quick self-check that shows where invisibility may be creeping in and which of the **5 Pillars of Agency** need the most attention right now.

From there, you can explore your Invisible Work Archetype and move through a short, guided **7-Day Archetype Reset Challenge** with simple prompts to help you shift patterns gently and intentionally.

Because choosing you isn't a someday thing; it starts right here and now.

Contents

Introduction

"Whatever It Takes"
—Imagine Dragons

How did I become so invisible?

You may not know the answer to this question, but that is exactly why I wrote this book. I want to help you answer that question and address that ache.

That flicker.

That wanting more that refuses to stay quiet.

And you likely picked up this book because you're feeling restless. You know that you were built for more than the life you've been negotiating your way through. You're tired of being competent and invisible at the exact same time.

Maybe, from the outside, your life looks fine. You're the reliable one. The supportive one. The capable one people come to when things need to be fixed. You get the promotion, you keep the family running, or you're the glue in every relationship.

Now, somehow, between all the roles you've played, you've started to fade as the main character from your own story.

It didn't happen all at once. And it probably wasn't dramatic. But was more like a quiet drift. A few swallowed sentences here, a few edited dreams there. A tendency to make yourself easier to manage, maybe easier to love. Over time, you became the person who holds everything together, while secretly wondering where *you* went and when you became invisible.

Choose You is my way of guiding you through that question, helping you understand how invisibility took hold and how to loosen it, without asking you to dismantle the life you've built to survive.

I'm not here to tell you that you've been doing life wrong. I'm here to name what happens when smart, thoughtful, big-hearted people slowly begin to disappear in the name of support, success, or survival. I'm here to help you see how invisibility creeps in dressed as goodness and responsibility, and how you can learn to become visible without burning down the life you've built.

You'll see parts of my story in these pages, and parts of your own.

You'll meet:

- The Invisible Child
- The Copy/Paste Teenager
- The Liberated, Lonely Young Adult
- The Supportive Spouse
- The Present Parent
- The Forgotten Grandparent

These are not case studies; they are mirrors for you at differing stages of life. These ways of being illustrate the many defenses we learn to use to tuck ourselves away long before anyone gives us a job title or a performance review.

Later on, you'll also discover the six **Invisible Work Archetypes**:

- The Overachiever
- The Pleaser
- The Always-On
- The Hurricane
- The Magnet
- The Placeholder

These archetypes each have their own rhythm and way of trying to keep you safe and valued in workplaces that often reward output more than authenticity. You may see yourself clearly in one of them, find echoes of yourself in all six, or notice them playing out in the people you work alongside.

Once we've traced how you got here and how those patterns show up at work, we'll walk through the **5 Pillars of Agency** designed to bring you back to yourself. You'll learn to:

- Remember Who You Are
- Find Your People
- Speak Up
- Start Before You're Ready
- Reset Your Perspective

These pillars are not life hacks. They're not a checklist. They're a sequence to walk through on purpose. You cannot speak up if you don't remember who you are. You cannot reset your perspective if you're surrounded by people who benefit from your self-doubt. You cannot move before you're ready if you've lost sight of what matters to you. Each pillar restores a part of you that went missing earlier in your story.

Along the way, I'll invite you to do more than read. I want you to take real action to move forward, and I've curated tools expressly for that purpose.

The tools that accompany this book are not extra credit, but are meant to be your companions.

At ChooseYouBook.com, you'll find the Invisible Work Archetype Assessment, which helps you see which archetype is running the show in your workday. After completing it, you'll automatically enter **The 7-Day Archetype Reset Challenge**, a short, practical email experience with daily prompts designed specifically for your archetype and to help you begin shifting patterns in real time.

Think of the assessment and the reset as conversation starters with yourself. They take this book from a "good read" that fades once life gets loud again and anchors the work you're doing here, giving you practical prompts, written reflections, and a personalized report you can return to and use beyond highlighted sentences and half-remembered insights.

Once you've built that awareness, there's a second step. The How Invisible Are You At Work? Quiz helps you reflect more deeply on how you're showing up across the **5 Pillars of Agency**: where you're strong, where you're holding back, and where your invisibility still has influence. You'll receive a personalized report for each pillar, with practical actions to help you move from awareness into choice.

Together, these tools mirror the work of real change: first seeing yourself clearly, and then deciding what you want to do differently.

Before we go any further, let me make you one promise.

Your life will not shift because I wrote this book.

Your life will shift because you're ready to stop defaulting to what's expected, start choosing what's true for you, and practice showing up differently in the moments that matter most.

You didn't open these pages to stay the same. You opened them to stop shrinking yourself to fit and start living in a way that feels honest again.

And you may not feel ready yet. That's okay. Most of us don't feel ready when we first realize how much of ourselves we've given away. Readiness is not the starting point in this journey, anyway. It grows as you take small, honest steps back toward yourself.

Here's what you can expect as you move through these pages:

In Part 1, "Where We Get Lost: Understanding Invisibility," we'll discuss how invisibility begins. Not in conference rooms, but at kitchen tables and in school corridors and quiet moments where you learned which parts of you were welcome and which were "too much." You'll appreciate how the child who learned to observe instead of speak, the teenager who blended in to avoid standing out, the partner who over-supported, and the parent who disappeared behind everyone else's needs all carry the same question: "Is there still room for me here?"

In Part 2, "How We Show Up: Unpacking the Invisible Work Archetypes," we step into the workplace and meet The Overachiever,

The Pleaser, The Always-On, The Hurricane, The Magnet, and The Placeholder in motion. Each archetype is explored through story, psychological insight, and practical guidance, advising you on how to work with this person and what to do if you *are* this person. You'll see that your habits at work are not random; they're connected to old survival strategies that once kept you safe and now keep you backstage. This is also where you'll be invited to take the Invisible Work Archetype Assessment and begin **The 7-Day Archetype Reset Challenge**, so your new information can turn into movement, not just awareness.

In Part 3, "The 5 Pillars of Agency: Returning to Who You've Always Been," you'll stop circling the problem and start building the life that fits you. You'll walk, step by step, through the **5 Pillars of Agency**. You'll remember who you are beneath everyone's expectations. You'll find (or re-find) the people who can help you expand instead of shrink. You'll practice using your voice in ways that feel grounded, not performative. You'll begin moving before you are fully ready. And you'll learn to reset your perspective so you're no longer limited by the lens you developed slowly, moment by moment, to make sense of your world.

The journey you're beginning here isn't about becoming louder or more impressive. It's about becoming honest with yourself, then aligning your life with that honesty, one decision, one boundary, and one conversation at a time.

If you're already wondering whether you're allowed to want more, let me assure you before we even get started:

- You don't have to be loud to be seen.

- You don't have to burn down your life to come back to yourself.

- You are allowed to outgrow versions of you that survived earlier seasons.
- You can take up more space than people are used to giving you.
- You can choose yourself without needing permission or consensus.

Take a breath.

You've already taken a brave action by picking up a book that asks you to look directly at your life. Let these pages be a conversation, not a verdict. Let them be a place where you tell the truth about yourself a little more than you have before.

And as you read, remember:

You are not starting from scratch.

You are starting from *you*.

Where We Get Lost: Understanding Invisibility

Chapter 1:

The Invisible Child

"Never Grow Up"
–Taylor Swift

It's been over three decades, and the details of that day are hazy. Was it a sun-drenched afternoon or a dreary, overcast one? I can't recall. But the classroom—ah, *that* I remember vividly. Grade 3, my desk was near the dusty window that was always streaked with rain, even on the brightest days. The teacher remains a blur, a nameless figure in the periphery of my memory. The other children? Faceless, echoes. All I retain with piercing clarity is the lead weight in my stomach, the frantic thump-thump-thump of my heart, and a suffocating sense of loneliness so profound it felt like a physical presence.

The recess bell shrieked, a joyous cacophonous tidal wave threatening to pull me under. Panic clawed at my throat. A desperate thought surfaced: *Stay. Just stay.* Back then, our schoolbags lived under our desks, no fancy cubbies for us. It made for the perfect hiding place.

The plan solidified in my nine-year-old mind. I would feign a frantic search for my lunch bag in a long, drawn-out charade. If the teacher didn't notice, I could be alone, truly and utterly alone, in the silent classroom.

I burrowed under my desk, rummaging theatrically, pretending to search for a non-existent sandwich. The exodus began. The scraping of chairs, the shuffle of feet, the muffled giggles of departing children. Each sound stretched into an eternity ... Time distorted and warped, every second expanding, until finally, blessed silence. Everyone was gone.

And then, a miracle. The teacher hadn't seen me. The door clicked shut. The reassuring thunk of the key in the lock sealed my solitary confinement, a sanctuary of solitude. The silence, once terrifying, now felt ... strangely comforting.

Being a locked-in child might be terrifying to some. For me, it was pure, unadulterated bliss. In that classroom, surrounded by the ghosts of absent classmates, I ate my lunch in peaceful solitude. I was alone, yes, but it was a vastly different kind of alone than the agonizing dread I'd felt moments before when picturing my loneliness on the playground. This was *good* alone. A quiet, safe, delicious alone. The relief was so utterly overwhelming, it's etched into my memory as vividly as if it happened yesterday. By choice, I was not standing there exposed with no one to claim me.

> *That moment branded me with a truth I carried for years:*
> *I would rather be alone than be seen alone, a preference*
> *born not of shyness but of self-preservation.*

Now, stay with me on the wayback bus a little longer ...

Let me whisk you back to the land of baby dolls and sparkly Barbies, a land ruled by glitter and the unwavering belief that sharing was indeed caring, even when it meant sacrificing your own perfectly combed Ken doll to a game of "hospital" orchestrated by a slightly tyrannical friend.

I was, shall we say, *excessively* kind. The kind of kid who, when three friends descended upon my meticulously organized playroom, promptly abandoned my cherished collection of porcelain dolls to dive into a raucous game of Candy Land, dictated entirely by the whims of five-year-old Tiffany and her unwavering desire to land on Gumdrop Mountain.

Lunchtime arrived whenever my guests decided it should. The carefully laid-out grilled cheese sandwich I'd anticipated was dwarfed by the culinary landscape of chips, cookies, and juice boxes my guests had brought.

As Tiffany, Brittany, and Jessica regaled each other with tales of their superior ponies and even more superior families, I sat quietly, nibbling a crust, my stories unspoken, my needs unnoticed. Left out. Not exactly a tear-jerking tragedy, but a small, persistent ache in my five-year-old heart, a seed of how to shrink myself planted deeply, nurtured by countless similar moments.

> **This wasn't a single incident; it was a pattern, a carefully woven tapestry of "me last," embroidered with pink thread and punctuated by the occasional sigh of quiet resignation.**

I never *wanted* to be the cause of anyone's unhappiness. The thought of someone feeling bad because of *me*? Unthinkable! So, I became the human equivalent of a Swiss army knife: adaptable, accommodating, and always, *always* ready to put everyone else's needs before my own.

I didn't possess superhuman empathy, but rather a hyper-developed sense of responsibility, a deep-seated desire to create a harmonious, happy little bubble for everyone around me, even if it meant my own happiness floated precariously on the outer edges. This wasn't a conscious choice so much as an ingrained behavior, a survival mechanism developed early on, one that quietly trained me to make myself smaller so that others could feel bigger.

That's just how it was. That's who I was. A cheerful, slightly frazzled, perpetually overlooked girl, whose happiness was measured in the smiles of others.

For a long time, I was okay with it. Or at least, that's what I told myself, until the quiet ache in my heart beneath the surface of my carefully constructed cheerfulness grew too loud to ignore.

Then came Grade 1. Picture this: Tiny me, armed with the misguided confidence of a child who believes their parents' friends' kids are automatically their BFFs. Spoiler alert: they weren't. "Friends of friends," it turned out, was a social loophole, not a friendship guarantee.

I was dropped into a world of pigtails and perfectly-pressed dresses, utterly friendless. And not for lack of trying. It was more like showing up to a dance without knowing the steps while everyone else moved in perfect sync. I lacked the necessary social dexterity.

Even when gently mocked (let's call it "low-key bullying"), I remained stubbornly placid. My maiden name? Bull. Yes, "Bull." Like the animal. You'd think that would be a deterrent. Apparently not. I was a particularly un-bull-y Bull, absorbing everything, even feeling sorry for the bullies! It was simpler to blend into the beige of the classroom, like a well-camouflaged chameleon.

Blending in wasn't just a classroom strategy; it became a way of life. And it stuck. This friendlessness persisted until I was 12. 12. Let that sink in. If you're a parent, you're probably experiencing heart palpitations right now. Birthday party invitations? Awkward, excruciating affairs. I was the wallflower mascot in boisterous gatherings, silently questioning if the hushed whispers of "What's *she* doing here?" were directed at my questionable party dress, a dress that, looking back, was perfectly fine. Those years stretched before me, a desolate road paved with my well-meaning but ultimately futile attempts at connection.

The irony? I was the queen of extravagant birthday celebrations. Jumping castles in preschool? Check. Two-night sleepovers? Absolutely. Nobody else had that kind of party. And yet, I was the invisible guest. I think my parents genuinely believed their daughter's birthday was a community outreach program. No one seemed to notice it was *my* birthday.

In elementary school, I perfected the art of silent, unnoticed existence. Teacher's pet? One hundred percent no. Class clown? Even less so. I was ... nothing. It's a peculiar talent, though one I wouldn't recommend mastering.

That shadowy space under my desk became my secret lair, which I frequented far too often. More than once, I found myself huddled amongst discarded worksheets, contemplating the existential dread of a forgotten nine-year-old. My teacher, bless her slightly bewildered heart, eventually noticed me, and then I was forced to go out to recess.

This invisibility clung to me like a stubborn dandelion seed. I often now wonder, *What if things had been different? What if that little girl, brimming with a light bright enough to power a small city, had been seen and found her tribe? Would she be a sunbeam-shooting, joy-spreading supernova by now? Or, at the very least, a slightly less anxious adult?*

> **It took me until I was 40, yes 40, to realize that I'd spent so much of my life as a silent observer, a spectator at the sidelines of my own life.**

Enter writing this book.

Choose You is not just about those solitary moments I spent under the desk, but the countless times I felt … unseen. And the truth is, I don't want anyone to live that way. Not a child, not a teenager, not a grown adult, and not you.

Under that desk, I thought I'd found relief, but I'd really found a loophole. When I chose solitude, it didn't sting; it soothed. The locked door didn't make me lonelier; it made me safe. I could breathe in the quiet and belong to myself for a minute.

That tiny trick turned into a whole operating system. If I could control the scene, I could avoid the humiliation of being the kid with nowhere to stand. So, I chose the classroom over the playground, my polite face instead of my real one, a smile over the risk of asking for what I wanted. I told myself it was kindness, harmony, and maturity. Sometimes it was. But more often it was concealment, a way to disappear without anyone noticing I was gone.

Here's the paradox of invisibility: "me last" becomes an identity as disappearing feels like courage, relief, and consideration. It even gets applause. But the bill always comes due, and one day, you realize you can't remember the last time you took up space without apologizing for it, or when you were chosen without first erasing pieces of yourself to make it easier for someone else.

Maybe you've adopted a similar coping tactic.

Perhaps you "offer" to stay behind and work through lunch so you don't have to navigate a noisy break room. You might RSVP "maybe" so plans can't reject you. Or your kindness is a decoy that keeps your needs out of the frame.

Two checks for you:

- Where do you choose smallness and call it "consideration"?
- Where does "keeping the peace" quietly cost you your place in the room?

If you recognize your younger (or even your current) self here, good. This isn't a problem to fix. It's proof that you know how to build safety. Now the work is learning how to assemble it without disappearing.

Chapter 2:

The Copy/Paste Teenager

"Bad Habits"
—Ed Sheeran

The year I turned 12 felt like the sun finally broke through a lifetime of overcast skies. Suddenly, there they were: *friends*. Not just classmates who tolerated my existence, but actual, giggling, secret-sharing, recess-racing companions. It was a revelation! The frantic squeals during the bell's final clang? I *got* it now. It was the sound of pure, unadulterated joy, the kind that makes your stomach flip not from nausea, but from exhilaration.

And then there was Jacky, a vision of midnight hair and alabaster skin: my person. We were inseparable, two peas in a perpetually giggling pod.

On the day of the fateful field trip that would change everything, the bus wound its way up a mountain road, each hairpin turn threatening to send my insides swirling. The scenery? A complete blur. My focus? Sharply trained on Jacky, my favorite human, nestled beside me.

The dizziness crept in gently, then hit like a wave. "Hang in there," I muttered to myself, envisioning the glorious fresh air that would surely save me upon arrival. *Hah.*

Stepping off the bus was like entering a funhouse mirror version of reality. Everything spun, blurred, and then bam! The urgent, undeniable need to hurl. My eyes darted wildly and found two choices stark and awful in their clarity: Jacky, or a cute boy who looked vaguely like a startled woodland creature. The choice, made in a nanosecond of pure, vomit-induced panic, was ... regrettable.

Let's just say that Jacky's pristine white shirt became a rather unfortunate recipient of my lunch. I didn't *want* to do it. In that moment, I had about as much control over my actions as a tumbleweed in a tornado.

"Why didn't you throw up in the empty space?" she shrieked, her voice a siren of betrayal. *An empty space? In the dizzying vortex of nausea?* I hadn't even *seen* an empty space, much less considered its vomit-receptive qualities.

That bus ride home felt longer than a lifetime. My stomach churned less from the lingering effects of the previous hour and more from the deep, gut-wrenching pain of a friendship shattered. It was my first heartbreak, a raw, painful thing that left me hollow and confused.

By 15, I was a walking contradiction. Yes, I had found new and loyal friends, some of whom remain my closest confidantes to this day, but the Jacky-shaped hole in my heart was a constant companion. I became two separate people, forever bound by the memory of that disastrous field trip and the lingering smell of regret (and vomit).

High school was a masterclass in average. Uniforms were a godsend, a disguise for the army of average. I wasn't bullied or exactly popular, just … invisible. My rebellion? Three earrings. Every Monday, one of the prefects would announce, "Candice, remove two earrings." Five minutes later, they'd be back in, tiny sparkling acts of defiance. Average height, average hair, average grades, average lunch.

I'd meticulously crafted a life of unremarkable ordinariness. It was exhausting. A never-ending chore of blending in, of not standing out, of dodging the dreaded spotlight. At school, I was the epitome of "meh."

But then … there was *the other me*. At 15, I discovered the Italian Club. If you haven't experienced the magic of a South African under-18 club, picture this: thumping bass, flashing lights, and the intoxicating scent of teenage freedom (alcohol-free, of course; drinking came later, at the ripe old age of 16).

Remember the family friends with the unhealthy obsession of Candy Land and the staged tyrannous rounds of "hospital" with my Ken doll? They'd grown up to be the cool girls of another school. The ones with shimmering eyelids, boyfriends with fancy cars and jet skis, the whole shebang. And somehow, they'd invited *me*—*Invisible Candice*—to party at the club. I had won the lottery of coolness.

I'd finally cracked the code and infiltrated the ranks of the effortlessly chic. I'd arrived. Or at least, thought I had. And in that moment, the Jacky-shaped hole in my heart felt a little less gaping, a little less lonely. The emptiness, for a few precious hours each week, faded into the background, replaced by the pulsating rhythm of the bass and the intoxicating sensation of belonging, if only for a night.

Getting my feet on that floor, though, was its own saga. Each outing required hours of exhausting negotiations with my mom, a back-and-forth of curfews, safety lectures, and promises I barely understood but swore I'd keep. Her face was a battlefield of sternness and grudging amusement, until finally she relented. "Fine," she sighed, the word a tiny victory in the never-ending war of teenage rebellion. "But one night only."

That first night ... the bass was a physical jolt, vibrating through my chest. I stood frozen, awkward as a newborn giraffe trying a tango, all knees and uncertainty. (*If you've ever read Giraffes Can't Dance, you know exactly what I mean.*) At first, I copied every move around me, a cut-and-paste version of cool; my arms lifted when theirs did, my hips swayed just enough not to look out of place.

Then, the music, an electrifying current of sound, pulled me in. I wasn't just hearing it; I was *feeling* it, a wave washing over me, smoothing out my shyness. My feet, clumsy at first, found a rhythm, a wobbly, joyous shuffle that transformed into something else. Something confident. Something *me*.

Far from the hallways of my high school, the Italian Club became my escape hatch, offering no judgment and no expectations. Just the safety of flashing lights and music so loud it drowned out doubt. In that darkness, I wasn't invisible; I was a blank canvas, finally free to splash bold strokes of laughter and messy, vibrant colors of joy.

Weekend after weekend, after getting a taste of the heady, addictive cocktail of freedom I craved, midnight loomed. My dad would usually pick me up. He'd pull into the lot around 11:30, and I knew if I wasn't there right away, he'd march straight up to the entrance. Mortifying. So, I'd bolt out the door, breathless, and lean into his window to beg, "Please, just one more song!" He'd nod his head, half acceptance, half exasperation written on his face, and I'd dart back inside for two more.

> **When the night finally ended, and I was safely next to him in the front seat, Dad queued up Shania Twain's "Man, I Feel Like a Woman!" for the ride home. He got me in a way only dads can.**

Laughing and dancing with reckless abandon, the newfound, effervescent me drew the boys in the way my brother always joked about—like cheese on a pizza. I attracted friends, laughter, and a whole heap of attention, making me feel *alive*.

At first, I just slipped out with the family-friends who weren't really friends at all, but the gatekeepers of the Italian Club world. Eventually, I let my three closest school buddies in on the secret, and soon they were joining me on Friday nights.

Next, the goody-two-shoes reputation I'd carried for years started fraying. My parents' liquor cabinet became my personal pharmacy for enhancing the intoxicating rush of "being me," and a desperate attempt to prolong the high. It started innocently enough: a shared beer with friends, the alcohol acting as a potent amplifier, turning up the volume on my inner disco ball to 11. Soon, "borrowing" alcohol became habit, the thrill of the heist adding to the intoxicating mix.

Underage, unsupervised, and gloriously, thrillingly drunk in the club bathroom, my friends and I would re-emerge to bounce off the walls and dance on the speakers until they threatened to collapse. We danced until our feet ached, our throats were raw from singing, and the music beat a rhythm deep within our souls.

> **It was reckless happiness, bottled in bass and sweat and laughter.**

Monday mornings found me back in my shell: the quiet, unremarkable girl. My assignments were always on time, yet never exceptional. I kept my hand down in class even when I knew the answer, gulping back my opinions before they had the chance to form. I didn't try; I just got by.

Two lives resided inside me, utterly distinct, yet undeniably *who I was*. No one suspected the electrifying transformation that occurred every Friday night. The mousy girl disappeared, and in her place danced a girl overflowing with joy, so alive that it spilled out of her every move.

Looking back, it's kind of heartbreaking, you know? This split personality thing was like keeping half of myself locked away in a closet, collecting dust bunnies and existential dread.

But hiding parts of ourselves doesn't just happen in high school. It can trail behind us for years, sneaking into boardrooms, relationships, and late-night thoughts when no one's watching. The world trains us to edit, mute, and cower, to choose acceptance over authenticity. And while it may feel like it's working in the moment—that you are safe—the cost is that you forget what it feels like to live as your whole self.

And if you're a teenager wrestling with a hidden brilliance (or hidden glitter cannons), listen up. I see you. You're not broken; you're rehearsing. Parents, please, for the love of all that is holy and teenage-angst-ridden, help your kids be *themselves*. Kids who learn they're allowed to show up as they are grow into adults who don't edit themselves, overcompensate, or burn out trying to belong.

In this crazy world of algorithms and perfectly filtered Instagram lives, authenticity is a rebellious act, and it's more vital now than ever.

Before you turn the page, ask yourself:

- Where did you first learn that being yourself might cost you belonging?
- What parts of you are still waiting for permission to come alive?

Here's to raising a generation of glorious, unapologetic weirdos and the adults who decide it's not too late to be one, too.

Chapter 3:

The Liberated, Lonely Young Adult

"Free Fallin'"
—Tom Petty

I would have changed my own diapers if I could have. That's how independent I have always been. Eighteen candles blown out, driver's license in hand, and boom! Four months after high school graduation, I was on a plane to London. My friend, Tiffany, the queen of the Italian Club, the girl who first thought I was cool enough to hang out with, came along for the ride.

London! Oh, London! We hit the ground running, or maybe stumbling, depending on how long we'd been at the pub. The sheer anonymity of that massive city was intoxicating, like wearing a magical invisibility cloak. But instead of hiding from Voldemort, I was mostly hiding from responsibility.

Finding a job was a comedy show. Back then, you *had* to read the newspaper, so every Sunday, we'd devour the classifieds and call every number, begging, "Will you hire us? Please? We're practically starving!" (Okay, maybe not practically, but boxed Fish Fingers get old real quick.) "No." "No." "No." "No." Rejection was our middle name for a few weeks.

My mom's threat echoed in my ears: "No job, no money, I'm not bailing you out, and you're coming home!"

"Over my dead body," I whispered to myself, reassuringly.

So, Tiffany and I ditched the phone, grabbed our maps (remember those?), and hoofed it across London. One train, then countless blocks later, and we had checked every place hiring. Tired but happy, we weaved through the busy London streets, determined to find jobs. After a long day of asking for a chance, we finally got lucky, and both landed jobs at a fancy five-star restaurant on Baker Street!

My parents were self-made millionaires. Seriously. From rags to riches, we lived the whole shebang. But "fancy" wasn't their style. We ate good food, sure, but five-star restaurants? Forget it. They'd probably choke on the prices. I'd been raised on simple meals, yet suddenly there I was, slinging wine in a London restaurant where the cutlery cost more than my rent. Wine, by the way, that I didn't understand in the slightest; I couldn't tell a white from a red, never mind a South of France *blah, blah, blah* from a Californian blend.

The customers were … intense. Think slick suits and even slicker hair. They'd order a Châteauneuf-du-Pape on a Tuesday, and I'd nod enthusiastically, praying it wasn't a soup. Once, I accidentally served a white wine *with a steak*. The man's face! It was like I'd insulted his grandmother. Or maybe his pet ferret. I'm not sure which was more precious to him.

I was a walking, talking sitcom. A charming mess, sure, but a mess, nonetheless. Spills were my signature move. Forgotten orders? My specialty. I once attempted a graceful presentation (think Olympic-level plate-placing), but gravity, that cosmic comedian, had other plans. In a dramatic flourish, the plate of slow-cooked beef and red wine tortellini landed squarely in the customer's lap. True story. My manager just hissed a world-weary sigh through his teeth that said, "You're employed because you show up, and I'm too tired to fire you."

Being demoted to breakfast duty was a gift from the gods. Coffee, juice, toast. Simple. Except for the day I faced the French press, a strange culinary weapon. One wrong push and coffee exploded all over me. I stood there dripping, beans clinging to my shirt, steam rising like I was a human kettle. The chef just stared, equal parts horrified and speechless, as if he couldn't quite believe anyone could mess up *that*. My life was a series of near-misses and epic fails.

My London adventures were legendary, bordering on mythical. Late nights, early mornings, blurry nightclubs, and the sweet, sweet anonymity of being unknown. I thrived in the crowds. If someone recognized me, I'd disappear into my shoes. Being "me" in London translated to being just another shut-the-club-down, fun-loving, taco-obsessed, nameless face on the night bus. It was glorious. It was freedom.

My parents, my friends, everyone who thought they knew best, none of them could control my life anymore.

London was my rebellion, my silent scream of independence.

It was my "you can't touch me" middle finger to the universe. And believe me, the very people who had boxed me in never saw it coming. This wasn't just a battle of wills; it was a full-blown war, and I was victorious.

Then my friend went home and poof! We haven't talked much since. But the best part? My older brother moved to London! I scored a two-bedroom apartment with four guys. No complaints; guys are low-drama. Living with my brother was awesome. He was the best support system. But the truth was, despite the amazing adventures I was having, I was lonely. Terribly, heartbreakingly lonely.

Picture this: My brother and his mates roaring with laughter, planning a pub crawl that involved questionable amounts of alcohol. I was that awkward extra person, the fifth wheel on a quadbike, the loser little sister tagging along. It stung. It really, really stung.

Outwardly, life was a whirlwind! I was having the absolute time of my life! I danced the night away in clubs, rode the night bus home singing off-key to '80s pop (don't judge), and even went to epic concerts, my favorite being "The Anger Management Tour," where, of course, I knew every word to every Eminem song.

I explored Europe, and in Amsterdam, got spectacularly, hilariously lost in a maze of identical canals. Until finally my Contiki tour group and I stumbled into our hostel just as the sun peeked over the horizon. I went to Egypt and marveled at the pyramids while narrowly avoiding over-enthusiastic camel owners pushing their "camel rides" a little too hard. Instagram gold before Instagram existed.

I cherished having my brother, but I didn't have *my* people. It was him and his friends ... and me ... a very enthusiastic, yet slightly lost appendage.

Moving overseas is life-changing in every way. The cruel twist is that you come back a different person, expanded, stretched, and rewired, while the friends you left behind stay the same. You no longer fit neatly into the puzzle you once belonged to. It's like finding a matching sock in the dryer only to realize it's been bleached pink. It technically fits, but it's not the same anymore.

When I got back from London, I had even fewer friends and even less in common with the ones remaining. I was invisible, embodying Rose in *Titanic* (minus the icy water and impending death, thankfully), "Screaming in a crowded room," completely unheard, the ultimate social outsider.

> **That's when it hit me: Invisibility doesn't always come from being ignored. Sometimes it comes from being changed in ways the people around you can't, or won't, see.**

Maybe you've felt it, too. You step back into a room you once belonged in, only to realize the room has moved on without you. The conversations feel foreign, the laughter doesn't quite include you, and suddenly you're more alone in a crowd than you ever were on your own.

Consider for a moment:

- Where have you outgrown a place or group that can't see the version of you that exists today?

- What part of yourself have you been retaining to squeeze back into an old box?

If these prompts or this chapter sound familiar, know this: You're not broken. You've grown. And growth always means leaving a part of you behind, even if it's just the illusion that being invisible is the safest way to be.

Chapter 4:

The Supportive Spouse

"Nothing's Gonna Stop Us Now"
—Starship

Let me set the record straight before we go any further: My marriage is not a cautionary tale. My husband and I are a team, a good one. Sometimes he takes the back seat; sometimes I do. This chapter is about the five-year stretch where it was my turn and what that did to me as a person. Spoiler: It didn't do me any favors.

Darryl and I got married in 2014. The ink on the marriage certificate was barely dry when I found myself in a maternity ward, six days shy of our first anniversary, with a squalling newborn in my arms. So much for a candlelit dinner in Paris.

Our anniversary gift to each other was sleep deprivation and a new relationship with topical solutions.

At the time, I was still firmly rooted in corporate life, with 10 years behind me and my identity tightly wrapped around being capable, reliable, and upwardly mobile. I took six months of maternity leave.

When I came back, the truth arrived fast and loud: I could not do both.

Back then, working from home wasn't on the table. Every day meant hauling myself into the office, baby safely dropped at daycare, and me trying to look like I hadn't just wrestled a car seat, a nappy bag, and traffic all before 8:00 a.m. My blouse carried the faintest trace of milk, my hair was pinned into something approximating "professional," and my inbox was already shouting before I'd had a sip of coffee. Evenings weren't any kinder: emails firing at 10:00 p.m., laptop glowing in the shadows while tomorrow's to-do list grew longer by the minute.

Something had to give. So, I gave.

I worked back my maternity leave, closed my laptop, and handed in my security badge. In South Africa, maternity leave covers four months, and because I took six, two unpaid, I was required to work back the full six months before I could leave. Ten years of climbing all reduced to a neat cardboard box. Eight days later, eight *days*, and there I was again, staring at a pregnancy test with two unmistakable lines. Cue the universe's laugh track.

> **I didn't pause the leap, though. I started building a consulting business anyway, reaching out to potential clients between naps, childcare logistics, and bouts of nausea.**

Belly first, 7-months pregnant, I walked into the biggest pitch of my career. A two-year contract. Multi-six figures. The kind of deal that could have changed everything. The boardroom fell quiet as I waddled—there's no graceful word for it—toward the projector, laptop clenched under one arm, nerves under the other. Chairs scraped, papers shuffled, eyes wandered from my face to my stomach and back again.

By the time I clicked to the third slide, I leaned in. "Let's *address the elephant in the room*," I said, flashing a cartoon elephant across the screen. "*It's me*." A ripple of laughter broke the tension. For about 10 seconds, I almost believed I'd closed the deal.

They didn't hire me. Thank goodness. I could barely get through the pitch without needing a nap. Our daughter arrived in 2017, right as we made the decision to move from South Africa to the U.S. Only the move didn't happen overnight. Darryl went first in stints, three weeks at a time, sometimes six. I stayed, toddlers at my ankles, one in half-day daycare, a nanny helping at home, my dad living a mile away, and swooping in for pick-ups when I had client calls. I had a village, and I will never deny that privilege.

But privilege doesn't cancel struggle. Two facts can be true.

I tried to hold onto a professional identity. "I'm a consultant," I'd say too brightly, the words tripping out of my mouth like they'd been rehearsed in the bathroom mirror. Then came the follow-up, every time: "Oh, *what kind of consulting?*"

That's when the wobble set in. My voice would dip, my sentences trailing off, as my eyes found the safety of my wine glass. I'd string together vague phrases like, "Some training work," or "A few projects here and there," hoping the casual inquisitor would nod and move on.

The truth was, I was making the equivalent of about $200 a month. Was that even a job or just an expensive hobby disguised as a learning and development strategist?

Although the asker would nod politely, I still caught their smile faltering, just slightly, like they could smell the hesitation and the fear that kept me from convincing myself. Of course, that same wobble followed me into bigger rooms, the ones where more than small talk was on the line.

Then slowly, almost undetectably, I went from independent to dependent, not because my husband asked it of me, but simply because that's how it unfolded. Asking him for money for a haircut or a new pair of jeans burned hotter than any corporate performance review ever had. Each small ask represented one more piece of myself slipping through my fingers.

Suddenly, March 2019. America. Nine pieces of luggage, two toddlers clinging like tiny, frantic barnacles, and the vast, crowded airport stretching before us. This was it. The Big Move. Except, there was no time to even blink at the enormity of it all. Just a frantic scramble.

The plane sighed onto the tarmac. Twenty-four hours? More like 24 lifetimes. The customs line snaked, a slow, agonizing beast. Then, our son, usually a whirlwind of energy, crumbled. His little legs, those tireless pistons of toddlerhood, simply gave up. He decided right then, right there, that sleep was the only option and flopped against his tattered puppy stuffie. Darryl and I became human sleds, inching forward, dragging our sleeping son like a reluctant, adorable fugitive. A security guard's sharp intake of breath confirmed our suspicion: We looked less like proud immigrants and more like people attempting a daring, if poorly executed, child heist.

Eventually, we were ushered into the glass room, a sterile, fluorescent box where suspicious travelers are observed for 45 minutes. Our babies wailed, their tiny voices shredded with hunger and fatigue, little humans unraveling under the harsh glare. This was our welcome. No gentle embrace into a new land, just hard plastic chairs and the silent judgment of strangers amid tears.

I'll spare you the play-by-play, but landing in America didn't mean we were done traveling. There was another flight, this time to Salt Lake City, more lines, more waiting, more logistics held together by adrenaline alone. While Darryl made three trips back and forth to the rental car with our luggage, I left our remaining bags with total strangers so I could take two exhausted toddlers to the restroom. At some point, we were finally in the car. Twenty-eight hours in and, instead of collapsing, we buckled up for one last stretch: a three-and-a-half-hour drive to the place that was now supposed to be home.

There was no family. No nanny. No safety net. Just us and our furniture, that monument to our new beginning (that, sadly, decided to take a scenic detour, arriving a glacial 14 weeks later).

Once settled in our new home, I got to work, wrestling with South African clients on Zoom calls at 4:00 a.m., my laptop glow painting my face in the pre-dawn gloom, the kids essentially living on trampolines—er, air mattresses. The clinking of cereal bowls in the kitchen was the soundtrack to my double life; the professional juggling act and domestic chaos were all powered by caffeine and stubborn will.

And then, as if life hadn't thrown us enough curveballs, my dad's chemo stopped working. Ten weeks after arriving at our empty, echoey house, I was back on a plane, two toddlers in tow, my heart cracking in real time. Six weeks later, I buried him.

Three days after the funeral, I was back in the States, the faint chemical sting of his hospital room clinging to my clothes, as if grief itself had soaked into the fabric.

Grief, at first, wasn't loud or dramatic, just a hollow ache, a gaping hole I couldn't fill. I was numb, my joy permanently switched off.

That summer blurred into a haze of sticky popsicle fingers and quiet surrender. I went through the motions, made snacks, folded laundry, and read bedtime stories, but everything was muted. I didn't sob at first; I just drifted. The heavy ache pressed against my chest.

My son's fourth birthday arrived, the same day my dad would have turned 70. The brutal contrast of celebration and loss fractured me. Back home, 100 people gathered to celebrate my dad's birthday, a testament to the man he was, even in his absence.

Here, on our side of the ocean, we threw a bounce-house party for my son. We invited his entire class and laid out colorful cakes and a riot of balloons. And … no one came. Not one single child from that class bothered to show up. A family friend eventually arrived, and a couple of kids from work tagged along, but the cavernous bounce house, meant to be a symphony of squeals and joyous chaos, was mostly just … empty. The tiny handful of children present had more than enough space to jump and fall without ever bumping into each other. A social void had opened up around us, a party of lonely echoes.

The next morning, Darryl boarded a plane. Suitcase rolling behind him, a quick kiss at the door, and then it was just me again, with two kids, a house full of deflated balloons, and the bounce house guy dismantling what was supposed to be joy. There wasn't a pause to ask how I was holding up. No moment of "Do you need me here?" We had made this choice together, and this was what that choice looked like.

That's when the numbness broke into uncontrollable crying. For two weeks, I cried through everything. Tears streaming as I buckled car seats. Sobs muffled in a towel while I bathed the kids. Silent tears tracing down as I spooned pasta onto their plates. At night, I'd read *Cave Baby* with a throat so tight the words came out as grating whispers. Even bedtime stories had become part of my grief.

When my husband finally walked back through the door, I tried to stand a little straighter, to look "fine." My face said otherwise: eyes swollen, skin puffy, voice scraped raw. *Please don't see me. Please do see me.* The thought looped in my head like a bad jingle.

He dropped his bag and froze. One look, a real look, and I saw it register. I wasn't the me he had married. I wasn't even sure I was me anymore. I'm just a zombie walking the kids from one room to the next, I caught myself thinking.

That single look changed everything. At the time, we were living in a small, rural town where the nights were so quiet you could hear Western movie soundtracks drifting from open windows, the kind of place that looks charming on screen and feels endless when you're breaking inside it. It wasn't a bad place. It just wasn't our place. We had no people there, no community to lean on, no room to exhale.

Darryl knew we couldn't keep living like this. Colorado wasn't a solution; it was a chance. We didn't know if it would make things better. We just knew we had to try something different. But this is the part that stung the most: Everyone called me "supportive" In so many words: "You're holding it together." "You're so strong." It was as if they were applauding me for disappearing, like my erasure was admirable. Inside, I'd evaporated.

I wasn't Candice anymore. I was Tristan's and Hayley's mom. I was Darryl's wife. I was the supportive spouse, the one whose name was dropped in conversations like an accessory: "She's supporting him."

Supporting my husband didn't mean he was shutting me out. Darryl always asked and always included me.

Taylor Swift's lyric, "*I'm the problem; it's me,*" played on repeat in my head. It was true. I didn't feel like I was contributing, equal, or even in the same league as him. Every time he booked a flight or made a decision, I told myself, *You're just along for the ride.* That inner voice chipped away at my confidence until I felt less than him on every front, even when no one told me I was.

For the first time in my life, I wasn't just invisible. I was gone.

Maybe your story looks nothing like mine. Maybe there are no moves across oceans, no toddlers or glass rooms at airports. But you've probably had a moment when you felt diminished next to your partner, friends, or colleagues. You've probably fielded a moment when you looked at your life and thought, *When did I become the supporting act in my own story?*

If you can relate to my experience, you're not alone, and you're not broken. Feeling "less than" isn't a flaw; it's a sign you've lost touch with your center. As I learned, painfully and slowly, finding your way back starts with noticing where you've disappeared.

Pause for a moment to answer these:

- Where have you been playing a supporting role when you were meant to be a full presence?

- What parts of you have gone quiet in the name of being supportive, strong, or easy to live with?

If those questions stir something, good. That's not self-criticism. It's awareness. And awareness is where your return begins.

Chapter 5:

The Present Parent

"I'll Stand By You"
—The Pretenders

I was the kid who traveled with a small nursery. Seven dolls lined up in a row, each one with a name, a bedtime routine, and a mother who meant business. Their plastic eyelids clicked shut as I "fed" them from tiny plates and tucked them in, blanket corners smoothed flat with serious concentration.

Even my Barbie had twins, then triplets, then quadruplets. Come on, Barbie, keep it together. Ken, please control yourself!

I loved order. I loved care. I loved love itself.

Years later, love arrived in a hospital bassinet, six days before our first anniversary. From 15 weeks, our son slept through the night—one of those rare parenting mercies people warn you never to brag about. Mornings were soft and rhythmic. Kettle whistles. Birdsong. My dad knocking on the door to check in. I'd spread a blanket on the lawn and watch chubby fingers grab at grass and ants, feeling a quiet contentment—but more I still can't quite describe.

Then came the decision that split me down the middle. I went back to work, the proud owner of a director title with a team to build and a strategy to shape. It was good work, the kind that lights up your brain and makes you feel sharp again. On paper, I was balanced. But in the calm between meetings and daycare pickups, another truth nagged: *I want to be there with my child now. Not after work. Now.*

So, I resigned on July 31st. Of course, our daughter was already on her way.

Two under two is not a parenting style. It's survival theater. The days blurred into a cycle of bottles, baths, bedtime stories, and more bottles. I learned to type with a baby sleeping across my chest. I could change a diaper with one hand and reheat cold coffee with the other. Some mornings, I showed up to client meetings in heels, blouse faintly scented in baby soap, pretending I'd slept. Other days, I'd take calls with a toddler wrapped around my leg, thinking, *You chose this, remember? You wanted this.*

> **Both thoughts were true. I wanted my children. I wanted my career. I just hadn't figured out how to want them both at the same time.**

When my husband started his airport-to-airport commute, work pulling him back and forth to mining sites as he and his business partner ran their industrial IT company, I stayed behind, holding together the home schedule with the precision of an air-traffic controller.

My younger brother would often pop in after work to help, offering an extra pair of hands for bath time, dinner time, anything to tame the wild chaos of bedtime with two toddlers. My dad would frequently be there, too, preparing dinner or cleaning the kitchen as I came down from putting Hayley to sleep.

Those 18 months became a blur of endings and beginnings: leaving my corporate role, starting a consulting business from scratch, having another baby, and learning how to run a household largely on my own while my husband was absent for four- to six-week stretches at a time.

Although I had help, I was still running a relay race and playing the part of every runner.

Somewhere in that 18-month blur, I had figured out how to double my old corporate salary.

I was proud to nail that accomplishment because I had worked for it, but those numbers only told part of the story. The real cost showed up during the day, when I was answering client emails while feeding small humans with one hand and typing with the other. It showed up in the quiet urge to read one more book, to be present, even when my inbox was already calling. And it showed up every morning, waking early with them, no matter how late I'd worked the night before, learning that success doesn't always ask out loud for sacrifice. Sometimes it just assumes you'll give it.

Little by little, I retreated; I didn't vanish. I just moved a few inches out of the spotlight so everyone else could shine. At first, it felt noble, then natural, and eventually it just was. I told myself it was what good mothers did: They make space. Until one day I realized I'd made so much space there wasn't much of me left standing in it.

Then came the move overseas. No work visa for me yet, which meant no new clients and no support system. I became the driver of small lives, school runs, soccer practice, gymnastics, and dancing lessons. The car was my office, my café, and my quiet place. It boasted crumbs in every crevice, spare hair ties looped around the gearshift, and a notebook on the passenger seat full of half-written ideas that began with ... "Someday."

I told myself it was temporary. *Hold on, Candice. Hold on.* But weeks turned into months, and months evolved into years before I'd even noticed.

> **Motherhood filled the hours, but something else hollowed them out. I loved my children fiercely, every story read, every skinned knee kissed, but there was always that incessant undertone: What about me?**

My laptop sat on the dining table, and I'd glance at it the way you spy on an ex on social media, curious, wistful, and guilty. I missed the version of me who built things that weren't made of LEGO®.

And still, of course, there was bliss. Always bliss in the form of sticky hands in mine at the crosswalk, unexpected laughter bubbling up in the back seat, and a sleeping child's head on my shoulder, heavy and warm. These moments were proof that love can be both an anchor and a weight.

Sometimes, though, the stillness after drop-off was deafening. I'd sit in the parked car for a minute too long, listening to the tick of the cooling engine, thinking *Other mothers would give anything for this time. Why can't you just be happy?*

> **People like to make parenting sound clean. They talk about sacrifice like it's noble and longing like it's betrayal. But real life is messier than that. Some days, I overflowed with love. Other days, I was leaking it from too many places to keep up.**

I didn't lose myself in one dramatic moment; it happened in microscopic ways. Every "I'll do it," every "It's fine," every "I'll just stay home this time." That's how you disappear, not through a single choice, but by a thousand tiny ones that all sound like kindness.

When I think back to the line of dolls on my childhood bed, all tucked in tight, I see it now for what it was: early training. I was practicing devotion. I was also practicing disappearance.

And maybe that's why this chapter was the hardest to write. Because I'm writing it exactly where my life happens: in the car, waiting for my son to finish soccer practice. The field lights are harsh, the windows fog up, and the smell of turf drifts in the cold air. I am overwhelmingly blessed to be here, to watch him run and grow. And yet, even as I sit in this car with my laptop balanced on my knees, I feel that small, relentless ache pulling me from who I am as a parent to who I am when I'm working.

I am both. And both can be true.

The strange thing about parenthood is how often we split it into camps: Stay-at-home. Working. Full-time. Part-time. As if love can be measured in hours. The truth is that both sides ache for what the other has.

When I was home full-time, I envied the business trips, the meetings, and the grown-up conversation Darryl was privy to. I longed for moments when someone would ask for my opinion instead of a snack. But I've seen the other side, too: the late nights, the hotel rooms that sink into silence after a day of pretending you're fine, the guilt that sits heavy on the chest of every working parent who missed another bedtime.

There's no winner here. Just two people staring across the same dinner table, each believing the other has it easier.

I think of my husband during those years of endless flights. He missed bath time, the giggles, the smell of baby lotion. He missed the tiny, ordinary things that make the hard days worth it. I got to be there for the first steps, the tooth fairy, and the school assemblies, but I also got to be there for the fevers, the tantrums, and the endless picking-up of small, discarded socks. That's what no one tells you: Presence comes with a cost, too.

For Darryl, the cost was absence. For me, it was erosion, the wearing away of the woman I used to be.

My husband missed moments he'll never get back, and I lost parts of myself I'm still learning how to reintroduce. Both of us were giving. Both of us were loving in the only ways we knew how. Both of us were trying to be the kind of parents our children would remember with warmth, not resentment.

Parenting isn't a competition of suffering. It's a series of impossible choices you keep making because there isn't another version of you available to live the other life.

Sometimes, when my husband talks about missing the little things, I can see it in his face, that flash of longing to rewind. And sometimes, when he looks at me across the room, I know he sees that same flash, flaring for different reasons. His ache is for the memories he missed. Mine is for the person I put on hold while everyone else moved forward.

We both gave up something to love the same people.

That's the unspoken truth most families know well. One parent gets to witness the milestones while the other parent works behind the scenes, making sure there's stability, security, and a home to come back to. Both roles matter and hold the weight of love.

Maybe that's what being a "present parent" really means. It's not trying to attain perfection or attendance; it's about intention. It's about showing up however you can, even if it means staying on that late-night call to make sure the bills are paid, or sitting in the car outside soccer practice, laptop open, trying to remember who you are beyond the pickup schedule.

So, if you're reading this from an airport lounge with your child's photo as your lock screen, know this: They feel your love, even from a time zone away. And if you're reading this from a parked car, watching from the sidelines of your life, understand, you're not failing by wanting more. You're human.

There's no easy version of this. There's only the version you choose today: a messy, beautiful, and complicated love. The kind that stretches you thin and fills you up all at once.

The kind where both parents, in different ways, learn to be present.

Two questions to sit with before you turn the page:

- What would change if you stopped treating your own needs as negotiable?
- What kind of presence do you want to model for the people who are watching you grow?

No call to action. No moral. Just a pause and a choice waiting quietly in the wings.

Chapter 6:

The Forgotten Grandparent

"The Way We Were"
—Barbra Streisand

One day, our little family, Darryl, the kids, and I, were at his business partner's place, actually, he's the kind of friend who's crossed the 20-year mark and feels more like family than anything else. It was one of those nights where the laughter flowed too easily, where the music was just loud enough to drown out pauses, where everyone was balancing paper plates on their laps and trying to talk over one another.

Somewhere between the clinking of glasses and round-robin stories, I noticed something impossible to unsee. My friend's mother, visiting for a few months, stood at the kitchen island, glass in hand, fully present and yet never quite entering the conversation. Every time she leaned in to speak, the moment moved on without her. She hadn't said a single word.

At first, I brushed it off. Big crowd. Different generation. Maybe she was just taking it in. But the longer the evening went on, the more her silence stretched, wrapping itself around her like an invisibility cloak.

A few months earlier, I'd spent time with her one-on-one. She had lived a *life*. Built a business from nothing. Supported a husband through illness. Divorced when it wasn't fashionable or easy. She was wise and wickedly funny, her laugh the kind that made everyone else join in. Her stories had depth and color and were textured like old film photos you can't stop looking at.

And now, here she was, quiet. Almost erased.

I remember taking a sip of my drink, the taste suddenly flat, and thinking, *Oh no. It follows us.*

This invisibility I'd been writing and talking about isn't just a phase of youth or marriage or motherhood. It doesn't dissolve with time. It can grip us for decades.

I smiled across the room and tried to catch her eye. She smiled back politely, stating without saying a word, "I'm fine, dear," then looked away.

That night, when we got home, I couldn't shake my realization.

I kept seeing her, not as a stranger, but as a mirror.

And then I thought of my parents.

My dad was never invisible. He couldn't be. The man had a gravitational pull; everyone orbited around him. Charisma wasn't a word we used growing up, but that's what he had in buckets. He was known. The guy you called when your car broke down, when your heart broke, when you needed to move a couch or start over.

At his funeral, there were almost 300 people. I stood there, numb, half-present, clutching tissues that disintegrated faster than my composure. People had waited for hours to speak with one of his children, and each one had a story to share with us.

"Your dad was the first one there when my wife passed away."

"Your dad visited me every single day in the hospital."

"Your dad helped me move when no one else would."

I remember thinking, Is *this what legacy looks like?*

A moment burned into me when I looked out over that crowd and thought, I *feel like a movie star just for being his daughter.*

The room blurred; my grief didn't. I could almost hear him saying, "See, Cands? This is what showing up looks like."

My dad never chased recognition, but he also never allowed himself to dwindle. He had this instinct to take up space with purpose and presence, not ego. He had filled that room by making others feel seen.

My mom is different. She prefers quiet nights, comfort movies, and her own company. She loves simplicity, order, and stillness. She's been everyone's support system. Always the helper, the listener, the one with the vodka and a listening ear—that's Mom.

Now, here's the question that haunts me sometimes:

When does support for others become self-erasure?

Mom's always been the backbone of everyone's story, but I wonder if anyone ever asked her to tell hers.

She would never complain, that's not her style, but I can see it in the pauses, in the way she brushes off compliments, in the way her stories start with "It wasn't a big deal."

But it *was*.

It always *is*.

And maybe that's what makes this chapter burn a little more—the realization that invisibility doesn't always come from neglect. Sometimes it comes from love—from giving so much that there's nothing left to hold you in place.

And then there's my mother-in-law.

We've talked for hours about life, sharing the kind of conversation that starts with a cup of tea and ends four hours later with cold mugs and full hearts. She's told me stories of the choices she's made, the dreams she's kept in her heart, the ways she poured herself into everyone else's future until her own became a sun-faded remnant.

She supported her husband through every storm, raised two incredible humans who actually want to spend time with her now, and built a home that feels like safety. And yet, beneath all that, I sometimes sense an unspoken what-if. I can detect the small moments of regret that creep in after decades of self-sacrifice. Those regrets grow roots, even in the soil of love.

> **Does one person really have to give up everything so another can thrive?**

My mother-in-law makes me wrestle with that question in the best way, reminding me that love and identity shouldn't exist on opposite sides of a scale. That maybe the win-lose dynamic is a lie we've been sold, and that being a partner or a parent doesn't have to mean always coming last, even when you love the people who come first.

She's taught me that balance doesn't mean 50/50; it means fluidity, and taking turns to lead, to rest, to dream.

I hope she truly knows how deeply I admire her. Even as she wrestled with her own invisibility, she became a guide for me. Proof that it's possible to give endlessly and still be worth being seen.

That's why this chapter is called "The Forgotten Grandparent."

It examines the people who have lived entire lifetimes, only to be shuttled along to the end of the table. It highlights those who have seen and survived events, who have built families and memories, and yet somehow, they have still disappeared in the noise of the young.

I've seen it happen at family gatherings. The young are loud, the stories are recycled, and somewhere between "Who's bringing dessert?" and "Pass the potatoes," the people who've lived the longest sit with their lips pressed together, waiting for their turn that never comes.

It's not malicious. It's just … life.

Life gets louder. They get quieter.

But it doesn't have to stay that way.

We don't lose our worth when our kids have kids of their own. We don't stop mattering because the world moves faster.

We stop mattering when we stop choosing to matter.

Being visible doesn't mean shouting. It means showing up as your full, imperfect, seasoned self. It means adding your stories to the mix. Saying, for example, "Oh, that reminds me …" then not apologizing for the interjection.

It means believing that your voice still belongs in the room.

Invisibility doesn't end when you retire or your kids move out. It ends the day you decide you're done disappearing.

I wish I'd sat beside my friend's mother that night. I wish I'd asked her to tell me one of her stories, the one about traveling the world alone, that impossible business deal she pulled off, or how she learned to live on her own terms long before it was normal.

Her story, like so many others, deserves to be heard.

That's what this whole book is about: Choosing visibility, even when it feels safer to be less noticeable.

If you take away nothing else from this chapter, let it be this:

You don't have to be loud to be seen.

You just have to be there.

Fully. Deliberately. Unapologetically.

So, at the next family gathering, tell your story. Laugh too loudly. Interrupt if you must. Be part of the noise.

Remember, invisibility doesn't leave on its own. It leaves when you do something about it.

Here's the truth this chapter confided in me as I wrote it: Invisibility isn't something life does *to* us. It's something we *begin to allow*. It doesn't arrive with fanfare or warning. It drifts in soundlessly, dressed as goodness, patience, kindness, and support. It looks a lot like love. And because of that, we rarely notice it settling in.

I think about my dad and how he never let invisibility take root. He showed up for people not because he needed to be the hero, but because showing up was his way of being alive.

I think about my mom and what it cost her to step back. Her work mattered deeply to her. Although my parents were partners in the business, my dad was front of house while she carried the back office, doing the unseen work that kept everything running. As she took up that supportive role, I could feel the weight of it in her quiet confessions. She didn't have to be loud with her feelings. I just knew. She carried a lot.

Watching her taught me something I didn't have words for at the time: that love can ask you to make yourself secondary and that doing so can leave an imprint of resentment even when it's done willingly and with care.

And I think about my mother-in-law, who has spent much of her life providing whatever the family needed in the moment, often without pause or complaint. Her support was generous and constant, and it came at a cost she didn't always name, though sometimes you could see it glance across her eyes.

What she taught me wasn't how to get it perfectly right, but how thin the line can be between being supportive and disappearing.

Watching her showed me that support and self *can* coexist, but only when we choose them consciously, not by default.

Maybe, as you've read this, someone who has spent a lifetime giving quietly, beautifully, almost invisibly—a parent, a grandparent, a mentor, or even yourself—has come to mind.

Now, take a moment before you turn the page. If you're considering someone other than yourself, remember them. Reach out. Ask for their story, or tell your own without rushing it, softening it, or editing it to make others comfortable. Speak in a way that invites attention, not approval. Every story shared adds a little more light and a little more life to rooms that have dimmed over time.

If you recognize traces of yourself here, try not to feel guilty about it. This is your awakening. It means you're seeing the places where you've softened into the background, and you're ready to choose something different.

Before you move on, pause long enough to answer this honestly:

- Where have you been telling your story in a way that keeps it palatable instead of true?
- What would change if you trusted that your voice doesn't need permission, polish, or consensus to matter?

Hold those questions loosely. You don't need the answers yet.

The next chapter will meet you between awareness and action and help you understand what invisibility really costs, so you can finally set that weight down.

Chapter 7:

The Weight of Invisibility

"Creep"
—Radiohead

It's a strange thing, realizing you've been fading, not dramatically, but in small increments. Knowing that you don't remember when it started, that there was no warning or single moment that announced, *You've disappeared now.*

It doesn't barge in one day, uninvited.

It creeps in disguised as goodness.

It arrives when we're praised for being easy, for not making a fuss, for being "helpful." At first, it feels virtuous, that warm pat on the shoulder that says, *"You're such a team player."*

You swallow your idea so someone else can shine. You stay quiet to keep the peace. You offer help instead of leadership, all because it feels safer.

It's subtle. It's applauded. And without noticing, it becomes muscle memory.

The scary part is how ordinary the dimmer switch turning down a fraction every year feels.

Until one morning you wake up and realize you've become the reliable one, the supportive one, and the background music to everyone else's highlight reel.

You catch yourself thinking, *When did my story become the backdrop to theirs?*

And yet, that realization, that sharp breath of awareness, isn't shameful. It's sacred proof that you're waking up. That you can feel the pulse of yourself again, faint but steady, insisting, *I'm still here.*

That moment is your invitation. You can rewrite it on your terms. You can choose visibility again, not the loud, performative kind that demands attention, but the kind that says, "I exist, and that's enough."

Choosing yourself doesn't have to mean *not* choosing anyone else. It's not selfish to want to be seen; it's a declaration that you belong, too. Every time someone steps into their fullness, they create permission for others to do the same. It's contagious, this kind of honesty.

I think about the times I've felt that dimming, the conversations where I've nodded instead of speaking, the projects where I stayed behind the scenes, and the moments when I told myself, *I'll get back to me later.*

But later rarely comes.

It waits without a peep in the corners of our lives until we decide to notice that it's time.

And when we finally do realize this truth, the weight of invisibility hits all at once.

> **You realize how heavy what no one asked you to carry really is.**
>
> **The expectations.**
>
> **The peacekeeping. The endless reliability that everyone applauds but no one reciprocates.**

It's hard to put down and hard to hold onto.

It's the weight of always being available but rarely being known. The weight of saying yes when your whole body wants to say no. The weight of realizing that somewhere along the way, your life became more about maintenance than meaning. That's what you pay when you keep choosing the background.

> **It takes your voice first, then your joy, and eventually, your reflection, until you can't recognize the person staring back at you.**

The grace is that noticing it isn't the end; it's actually the beginning. It isn't guilt. It's resurrection. It's the silent rising of the parts of you that refused to disappear completely, waiting for you to notice them again. That's where your story begins anew, in the decision to stop carrying the weight alone. You can put it down, pound by pound, and choose visibility in an unfiltered laugh that escapes before you can stop yourself, in a calm moment where you let yourself be fully seen. It's not about taking over or making noise; it's about not apologizing for existing.

Take a slow breath. Feel the weight of it, not to judge it, but simply to notice where it lives. Maybe you can detect it settled in your shoulders and how they tighten without you realizing. Maybe it lingers in your calendar, that endless stretch of commitments and expectations that leaves little room for you. Or maybe it's there in the familiar pause before you speak, when you think, *It's fine. I'll just let it go.*

Whatever shape it takes, this weight isn't proof that you've failed. It's proof that you've cared deeply, fiercely, and often without making a fuss. You've been trying to hold the world steady for everyone else, which is beautiful feedback about who you are.

As you commit to reappearing, remember that caring doesn't have to mean disappearing. You can love and support people and still keep yourself in the picture. These two concepts aren't opposites. They can coexist.

Before you turn the page, make yourself a promise. The next time you feel that familiar urge to shrink back and smooth things over or to insist it's fine when it isn't, pause, just for a heartbeat. Ask yourself:

- *What would it look like if I stayed?*
- *If I spoke?*
- *If I didn't step aside this time?*

The weight lifts in moments of staying true to yourself, through one single pause, choice, or visible breath at a time.

Part 1 Recap

In Part 1, we explored the many ways invisibility can weave itself into our lives; we delved into the moments when we step back, dial down our light, or mistake being agreeable for being kind. We saw how our beliefs can start early, how they follow us through relationships, parenthood, and love and loss, until they become second nature.

We also learned that invisibility doesn't clock out when we go to work. It comes with us into meetings, into decisions, into every room where we hesitate to speak up. The patterns we learn in life are the same ones we carry into our careers, and the way we disappear in one space often resembles the way we disappear in another.

What's in Store: Parts 2 & 3

In Part 2, we'll step into the workplace. I'll introduce you to the world I live in, the people I work with every day, and the place where I, possibly like you, spend most of my waking hours. Be aware, as you keep reading, that the same habits that make us invisible at home can, without much fanfare, erode our presence at work. The same fears that keep us from speaking up in a meeting are the ones that keep us from being seen in our own lives.

> **And yet, I believe deeply, fiercely, that work doesn't have to drain us.**

We can *love* what we do. We can wake up on a Monday morning excited for the week ahead, proud of what we contribute, and energized by the impact we're making.

When we're happy at work, this joy spreads outward. We bring it home. It shows up at our dinner tables in the stories we tell our kids, in the laughter we share with friends, and in the way we support our communities. Joy is like an overturned water glass, trickling into all the areas that matter in our lives. It fuels visibility and makes us fully present, confident, and alive in the spaces where we spend most of our time.

Here's another twist on what we've been talking about: We don't just vanish by staying quiet. Sometimes, we overcompensate. We push harder, work longer, control more, or speak louder, all in an effort to be seen, respected, or safe. These are the patterns we slip into when we're out of alignment with ourselves, when the weight of invisibility follows us into the office, the meeting room, or a Zoom call, and we start overcompensating instead of being.

In Part 2, we'll hold a mirror up to those versions of ourselves. We'll learn to recognize the disguises invisibility wears, so that when we see them on others, we'll know how to help lift each other out of the shadows.

Work isn't just about what we do; it's about who we are *while* we're doing it. That understanding will lead us into Part 3, where you'll be given the tools to discover how to find yourself again in the middle of the chaos, noise, and constant pressure of everyday life.

But first, let's talk about the patterns we bring with us and how they support the archetypes we may be living each day.

PART 2

How We Show Up: Unpacking the Invisible Work Archetypes

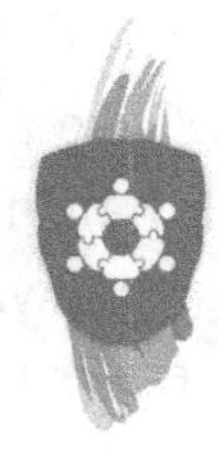

Chapter 8:

The Work Archetypes Explained

"Human"
—Rag'n'Bone Man

We've met the parts of ourselves that duck and weave, puff up like startled pigeons, or blend into the wallpaper just to keep the peace. Invisibility lives in our thoughts and childhood stories. It's not a private, behind-the-scenes act. It's a full-blown production playing out under the harsh fluorescent lights of our workplaces.

Think about the late-night emails you write with a hint of desperation disguised as efficiency. The cheerful "Sure, I can take that on," dropped into a chat window even though your plate is already overflowing. The carefully practiced smile you bring to every meeting, convincing enough to fool everyone but you and a work bestie.

These moments might seem small, isolated even, but they're not. They're patterns, and as anyone who's ever tried to untangle a knotted necklace knows, patterns, especially the stubborn ones, always have roots.

When I first started noticing these behaviors, I wasn't even looking for them. It was like stumbling into a secret club I hadn't realized I'd joined. Over the years, I've had hundreds of conversations in coaching sessions, workshops, hallway catch-ups, and moments after a session ends when someone stays behind, waiting until the room clears before asking, "Can I tell you something?"

There were no clipboards, no surveys, no white lab coats. And then I remembered one of my first lectures in Psychology, sitting in a crowded university hall as we talked about human behavior in neat theories and tidy models, never quite naming the quiet truth beneath them: that people can do everything "right" and still feel that something isn't quite right.

Years later, after studying how humans think, adapt, and behave inside systems designed to shape them, I could finally see it clearly. What I was hearing in those hushed after-session confessions wasn't anecdotal or accidental. It was patterned. Predictable. And deeply human.

After a while, the similarities in the human experience became impossible to ignore. Different companies, different job titles, all with the same ache in common. The same relentless drive to prove worth. The same carefully constructed strategies to stay safe, to be seen, to belong. The same exhaustion that creeps in when we confuse busyness for value and approval for connection. What started as a few shared experiences eventually took shape as something more; a map of how invisibility shows up in our work lives emerged.

Which is how the **Invisible Work Archetypes** were born. They didn't come from clinical studies, diagnostic manuals, or personality frameworks, though they are informed by my formal studies in Psychology and Organizational Psychology. What shaped them most, however, was lived experience. Years spent inside organizations, developing tens of thousands of people across roles, functions, and industries.

I've held positions from administrative and director roles to leading enterprise-wide capability and transformation work, partnering directly with executive teams in organizations ranging from 50 people to tens of thousands. I've been in the room as the facilitator, the strategist, and the participant myself. And across all those contexts, the same patterns kept surfacing: people navigating ambition and belonging in workplaces that often reward output over authenticity.

Linking the Invisible Work Archetypes to Popular Assessments

If you've spent any time in personal or professional development, chances are you've encountered at least one personality or behavioral assessment along the way. Tools like the Enneagram, the Big Five, DiSC, or CliftonStrengths have become familiar reference points in workplaces, coaching conversations, and leadership programs. Each of them emerged from different traditions in psychology and organizational development, and each offers a useful lens on human behavior.

The Enneagram, for example, focuses on core motivations, fears, and the internal drivers behind behavior. It helps people understand *why* they react the way they do, especially under stress or security.

The Big Five, widely used in psychological research, looks at broad personality traits such as Openness, Conscientiousness, and emotional stability, offering insight into consistent behavioral tendencies over time.

DiSC centers on observable behavior and communication styles, helping people understand how they tend to act in relation to others.

CliftonStrengths takes a different angle altogether, identifying natural talent patterns and highlighting where individuals are most likely to thrive when working from their strengths.

> *Each of these tools is valuable. Each offers a snapshot, not a full portrait. And none of them claim to capture the entire complexity of a human being.*

The **Invisible Work Archetypes** sit alongside these frameworks, not in competition with them. Where many assessments explore who you are or what comes most naturally to you, these archetypes focus on something more situational: how you've learned to operate in your work environment. They surface in the strategies people adopt to stay safe, useful, respected, or indispensable, often without realizing they're doing it.

That distinction matters. Because invisibility at work is rarely about personality alone. It's shaped by context, culture, expectations, and power.

> *The same person can show up very differently depending on the environment they're in, the leaders they work under, and the signals they've learned to respond to over time.*

These archetypes are not labels to collect or boxes to climb into. They are mirrors. Ways of recognizing patterns that may have once protected you, helped you succeed, or kept you included, but that may now be costing more than they give.

As with any framework, the value lies not in being "typed," but in what you choose to do with the insight. That's where we'll go next.

Work Archetypes

Each archetype I have developed offers a window into how you may be operating invisibly at work. It highlights the ways you protect yourself in environments that don't always feel safe or allow you to be fully human. Some of these patterns may have once served you well; they helped you fit in, succeed, and survive. But over time, these same protective methods became the very habits keeping you stuck, unseen, or completely spent.

In the pages that follow, you'll meet six of these archetypes:

- **The Overachiever**
- **The Pleaser**
- **The Always-On**
- **The Hurricane**
- **The Magnet**
- **The Placeholder**

You might recognize yourself in one or two of these archetypes. And if you're having one of those weeks where everything feels a bit much, you may see flashes of yourself in all six. That's okay. These avatars aren't about labeling yourself, but about recognizing the roles you've unconsciously stepped into.

The great news is, once you can see the role you're playing, you can choose a new one. That's the real power awaiting you in Part 2.

Buckle up and explore each archetype, its roots, behaviors, and the hidden cost of staying in that pattern. Then we'll begin to uncover what it looks like when you finally step away from the habits that are keeping you from stepping into the person you are meant to be.

Invisibility isn't your ending. It's the signal you need to see before you can embrace the spotlight, this time, fully yourself.

Chapter 9:

The Overachiever

"Unstoppable"
—Sia

The blue light of the laptop screen was the only ambience in Anya's otherwise dark apartment. It was 9:47 p.m., a time when most people were winding down, catching up on a show, or scrolling through cat videos. Anya, however, was knee-deep in a report. Not just a report, the third revision of one her manager had already called "great."

He'd said it that afternoon, smiling. "This looks great, Anya."

She'd smiled back, polite and even. "Thank you."

The moment his back was turned, she'd reopened the document.

"Great," she scoffed to herself. The word was stale bread. For people who settled for "good enough."

Anya didn't do "good enough." She did "so astronomically better than anyone else expects that they won't even know where to begin to criticize it."

Somewhere between adjusting the alignment in cell G42 and color-coding a pie chart no one had asked for, or could probably read, she promised herself that this would be the last tweak. *Just one more.*

But one more turned into an hour. The only sounds were the steady hum of her laptop and the faint crack of her desk chair when she leaned back. The pang between her shoulders had become a nightly companion, her body's way of reminding her that while her mind was still sprinting, the rest of her had clocked out long ago.

Tomorrow, someone, probably Brenda from accounting, the one who always talked about her petunias, would shake her head with a small, knowing smile and say, "Anya, I don't know how you do it all."

Anya would laugh softly, shrug her shoulders, and wave it off.

The truth? *She didn't know either.*

All she knew, all she felt was that gold stars were her oxygen, and lately, the air was getting thin.

How to Recognize The Overachiever

If "driven" were a person, it would be the Overachiever. Overachievers are the ones whose calendars look like precarious towers of overlapping meetings, who volunteer for a new project before the pitch is even finished, and whose "quick updates" somehow evolve into mini-presentations.

Overachievers are the steady pulse of the workplace; they are competent, relentless, and often exhausted, although they'll never let you see it.

Their speech is laced with qualifiers. You'll hear phrases like "I'll just finish this," "I should probably double-check," or "Let me tighten it up a bit." Overwork isn't a problem in their world; it's proof of pride. Their favorite phrase, the one that captures their entire operating system, is "Best practice isn't good enough."

To The Overachiever, "good enough" sounds like mediocrity. They don't compete to win; they compete to *deserve* the win—a critical distinction. They'll triple-check a slide deck, adjust the spacing in a paragraph, and rewrite an email because it didn't feel right. Once they meet the standard, they quietly move the goalposts and start again. Their drive is endless, but so is their restlessness.

Why Overachievers Are the Way They Are

At their core, The Overachiever's need is heartbreakingly simple: to be good, to be competent, to be worthy. Somewhere along the way, they learned that love, praise, and even safety were conditional, that being right, polite, productive, or helpful was the surest way to be accepted. Over time, that lesson hardened into a belief: *I am what I achieve.*

Their deepest fear isn't failure; it's being seen as lazy, wrong, or unworthy. For them, invisibility doesn't look like being ignored; it looks like being ordinary. So, they push harder, run faster, and perfect everything they touch, mistaking motion for meaning.

It isn't arrogance that drives The Overachiever; it's protection. As long as they are "doing," they can't be accused of not being enough.

The tragedy, of course, is that their effort rarely brings peace. The bar they're chasing keeps moving, always just out of reach. The applause peters out, replaced by the next expectation, most of which they set for themselves.

The Link

If you laid The Overachiever's wiring across the best-known frameworks like the ones I am detailing below, their picture would look remarkably consistent.

In the Enneagram, they're the love child of Type 1, The Reformer, and Type 3, The Achiever. Type 1 brings that deep moral perfectionism, the need to be right, precise, and principled. Type 3 adds the performance drive, the need to be admired, productive, and exceptional. Together, they create someone who flinches at anything less than excellence and shouts, "You're only as worthy as your results!"

The Big Five paints a similar portrait: sky-high Conscientiousness, a person disciplined, focused, and methodical, paired with a wisp of Neuroticism. They hear the unending brain rattle of "Could I have done more?" And it never quite evaporates, even after success.

Next, step into the DiSC model, and you'll see that their energy lights up the D quadrant: Dominance, meaning they are decisive, determined (and allergic to inefficiency). To an Overachiever, "good enough" can even feel like failure in contrast to precision and speed—the twin currencies of respect.

And in CliftonStrengths, their themes read like a resume of relentless motion: Achiever, Responsibility, Focus, Discipline, Maximizer, Analytical, Strategic, Futuristic, Competition. They see possibilities, build plans, and execute flawlessly. They're not just finishers;

they're architects of ambition. When their strengths are balanced, they lead teams to new heights. But when the dial turns too high, that same brilliance morphs into burnout, causing a never-ending loop of achievement chasing validation.

Every framework they live out in the workplace tells the same story: Drive without pause, excellence without ease. The Overachiever is innately suited to climb mountains, although they rarely pause long enough to look up and realize they're already standing on the peak.

How to Work Alongside The Overachiever

Overachievers don't need more motivation; they need permission. They already bring enough drive for three people. What they lack is space, permission to stop, to breathe, and to decide that *finished really means finished.*

If you manage or collaborate with them, set clear boundaries around what "done" looks like. They'll keep going until you tell them to stop. Praise their progress as well as their results; they tend to discount any compliment that isn't backed by a measurable achievement. Assign projects that stretch their thinking rather than their hours, and model the behavior you want them to believe is possible.

> *The Overachiever won't trust balance until they see someone they respect modeling it.*

When you tell them, "This is good," say it once and mean it. When you say, "Go home," insist they beat feet already. You are not stifling their potential; you're giving them back their humanity. Without you setting parameters, they won't be able to help themselves, which doesn't serve them or anyone else on the team who has grown to rely on them.

What If You Are an Overachiever?

If you saw yourself in these pages, take a moment to sit with that realization. The tightness you feel in your chest, that flutter of guilt or defensiveness, is simply the part of you that's tired of earning your right to exist.

> *You are not your deliverables. You are not your inbox. You are not the completion rate of your to-do list.*

The Overachiever archetype is built on a beautiful lie: *If I just do enough, I'll finally feel enough.* But "enough" isn't a destination you reach through effort; it's a decision you make through awareness.

To make a change and reclaim your life from the unattainable goal of reaching perfection, start small. Send an email without rereading it three times. Finish a project before it's perfect. Let someone else's 80% stand, even when you know you could make it better. Rest *before* you earn it. You'll be amazed at how little the world changes when you stop pushing quite so hard. And even when things don't go exactly to plan, you'll discover something just as important: You're still standing, still trusted, still okay.

> *Success does not have to hurt. Excellence does not require exhaustion. The next time you're tempted to open that file one more time, remember: You don't have to earn your worth through your work. You already have it.*

Your Next Step

If this chapter felt a little too close to home, don't stop here. Awareness is the first step, but it's what you do with it that changes everything. You don't have to figure it out alone. I've created a free Invisible Work Archetype Assessment to help you identify the archetype shaping how you show up at work. From there, you'll be guided through a short, **7-Day Archetype Reset Challenge** with simple, practical prompts designed to help you loosen patterns and create a little more breathing room.

Take the assessment, and start your reset at ChooseYouBook.com.

Your visibility begins the moment you pause long enough to see yourself clearly and recognize that you are already enough, without doing more, fixing more, or proving more.

Chapter 10:

The Pleaser

"You Don't Own Me"
—Lesley Gore

Eli's inbox chimed, each notification a tiny tap against his already frayed nerves. Another email. The subject line read: "URGENT: Quick Question about Project X." His stomach did that familiar, unpleasant flip. He hadn't even finished the report from Monday's "quick favor" for marketing, the one that had swallowed his lunch break whole. Still, the sender's name nearly shouted at him, a senior colleague. A direct ask.

He opened it. The tone was polite, almost apologetic: "Eli, so sorry to bother you, but would you mind taking a quick peek at this? Just need a fresh pair of eyes before it goes out."

A "quick peek" always turned into an hour-long deep dive, full of detailed feedback and, somehow, a few extra tasks that weren't his to begin with.

The words left his fingers before he even thought about them: "Of course, happy to help!" He pictured the sender's relieved sigh, his gratitude palpable through the screen. It was a warm rush, yet fleeting, like a ray of sunshine on a cold day—which is why he chased the feeling on the reg. Then the chill would set in again. The undone items on his list would loom even larger, a silent mountain he'd climb after everyone else had gone home.

He'd tried once to draw a line, exercising a polite experiment in boundaries. A colleague had called with a last-minute request, and he'd said carefully, "Perhaps later this afternoon?" The pause on the other end was thick with disappointment. "Oh. Okay," the voice had said, and the sound of it had made his shoulders creep up to his ears. Within minutes, he'd sent a follow-up message offering to handle it right away. The knot of guilt had loosened briefly, replaced by the familiar fatigue of overcommitment.

Later, picking at a sandwich at his desk, Eli had looked up as Sarah from accounting breezed past. "Eli, you are a lifesaver! Thanks again for staying late yesterday." Her gratitude was genuine. It should have felt good. Instead, it was heavy, another brick that Eli was quietly using to build a wall made of other people's solved problems around himself. His own work, the quarterly review he'd meant to polish that afternoon, sat untouched. The thought of presenting it half-finished made his skin prickle.

Eli's phone buzzed. Another ping. A message from a colleague in another department, asking for feedback on a design mock-up. His fingers hovered over the keyboard. The harmony of a well-oiled team that saw him as indispensable was a delicate melody. And Eli? He was the conductor, determined to keep every instrument playing in perfect tune, even if it meant his own violin stayed silent, gathering dust. The thought of dissonance, of his "yes" ever becoming a "no," made his head hurt.

Better to keep the music going. Better to be the one everyone relied on. Better to please.

How to Recognize The Pleaser

The Pleaser is the heart of every workplace. The steady pulse that keeps things moving, smoothing strain and filling gaps before anyone else notices. They're the first to comfort, the last to complain, and the oil that keeps everything running.

You'll often hear The Pleaser say things like, "It's no trouble at all," or "Whatever works best for the team." They speak in reassurances, constantly scanning for signs of discomfort: a furrowed brow, a sigh, a silence indicating someone's upset that they rush to fill with helpfulness, empathy, and extra work.

> *The Pleaser hands out "yes" like candy, hoping sweetness will keep the peace. But inside, resentment simmers.*

They wonder why others don't notice their effort, or why appreciation always seems just out of reach.

To The Pleaser, conflict feels dangerous, and boundaries are rejection. They'd rather quietly drown than risk being called difficult.

Why Pleasers Are the Way They Are

At their core, Pleasers need to feel needed. Their fear, often unspoken, is that if they stop giving, they'll stop mattering. Somewhere early on, they learned that being helpful kept them safe and being agreeable kept them loved. It's not that they don't have opinions or needs; they've just spent years tucking them behind kindness and diplomacy.

Their sense of worth is built on how much they can give, how easy they can make life and projects for others, and how well they can file down rough edges. They thrive on belonging, but it's a fragile belonging, one that depends on constant self-sacrifice.

To The Pleaser, saying no doesn't feel like setting a boundary. It feels like closing a door on connection. So, they keep saying yes, mistaking self-erasure for generosity.

The Link

If you've ever taken a personality assessment, you can probably guess where Eli would land. Picture the classic office icebreaker: a group huddled around a whiteboard, jotting down Enneagram types and DiSC letters like secret codes. Eli's results would draw a knowing smile from everyone in the room. "Oh, of course you're a 2," someone would say. "You're The Helper; that tracks."

And it does. Eli wouldn't argue. He's built his reputation on being exactly that. But somewhere beneath the nod and the half-smile, a thought lingers that he would never voice: *There's more here than what they're naming.*

In the Enneagram, The Pleaser is likely a blend of Type 2, The Helper, and Type 9, The Peacemaker, equaling the perfect storm of compassion and calm. Type 2s long to be appreciated, to feel that their care has impact. Type 9s crave harmony and connection, often going quiet to keep the peace. Put them together, and you get someone like Eli: the kind of person who apologizes when *you* bump into *them.*

In Big Five terms, Pleasers would likely score high on Agreeableness and empathy. They're the ones who anticipate needs before they're spoken and remember how you take your coffee, even if you forgot theirs. But that same empathy, when left unchecked, turns into emotional overextension. They absorb tension the way an inbox absorbs unread emails. Silently. Constantly. Until one day it's overflowing and they're left wondering why they're exhausted.

Their DiSC profile would sit firmly in the S/i-S quadrant: reflecting Steadiness, meaning they are supportive and relational. These are the team members who keep the peace not by stepping forward, but by softening the edges afterward. They absorb discomfort, smooth relationships, and make it easier for everyone else to carry on.

And in CliftonStrengths, their top themes would read like a love letter to connection: Empathy, Harmony, Developer, Includer, Adaptability, Positivity, Relator, and Individualization.

> **Pleasers see people not as data points, but as stories.**

They adjust their tone, their timing, and their needs to make others comfortable. When these strengths are balanced, they create workplaces that feel safe and kind. But when they tilt too far in their generosity, Pleasers become invisible.

> **Across all models, the pattern holds steady: The Pleaser's gift is emotional intelligence; their trap is emotional depletion.**

How to Work Alongside The Pleaser

Pleasers need appreciation, not pity. They thrive when their kindness is acknowledged and when they're invited to express opinions safely. If you lead or collaborate with a Pleaser, the most valuable thing you can do is ask what they want, and then wait for the real answer. If they are a little slow to be honest with you, encourage them to speak up, and let them know you appreciate them.

> **Don't just thank them for doing more; thank them for speaking up, setting limits, or saying no. Make it clear that disagreement isn't disloyalty, it's maturity.**

Encourage them to prioritize their work without guilt, and model boundary-setting yourself.

When you see them taking on too much, step in with firm reassurance: "You don't have to carry this alone." For a Pleaser, permission to pause is the ultimate act of care. Letting them know that their boundary-reinforcing won't cause disruption or be seen as disloyal is paramount to help them move past stagnation.

What If You Are a Pleaser?

If this chapter feels a little tender, it's probably because you've spent years measuring your worth in "thank yous." And feeling the punch if you don't hear one. You've learned to read the room before you read yourself. You've mastered the art of keeping everyone comfortable, except you.

Here's what you need to know: Saying no doesn't make you unkind. Asking for help doesn't make you selfish. You are allowed to exist outside of other people's needs.

To make a change, start with a manageable action. Pause before you automatically say yes. Ask yourself, *Do I want to do this, or do I just not want to disappoint?* Let the silence hang for a moment;

it's not rejection. It's space. You can still be kind without constantly being available.

> **You can still be loved without always being needed. The people who truly value you don't require your exhaustion as proof of your worth.**

You've spent so long keeping the peace that you may have forgotten: Your voice matters, too. Learning to use it again might just be the most generous thing you ever do for yourself and for everyone else around you.

Your Next Step

Realization is not a reason to stop, so keep going with your transformation to become the more balanced person you've always wanted to be.

Start your **7-Day Archetype Reset Challenge** today by completing the free Invisible Work Archetype Assessment to discover which pattern most shapes your workday. It's a short, practical journey that can help you practice saying no without guilt and yes without resentment.

Your visibility doesn't come from keeping everyone else comfortable. It begins the moment you remember that your boundaries and your voice deserve space, too.

Chapter 11:

The Always-On

"Good as Hell"
—Lizzo

Sam didn't just walk into a room; he changed it. The air always lifted with a spark of anticipation when he showed up, as happens the few seconds before your favorite song starts to play. Meetings that usually dragged suddenly felt alive when Sam took a seat at the table.

He was the human version of that first sip of coffee in the morning, or the smell of freshly baked bread drifting from a café. Even on gray days, it was as if he brought his own sunlight with him: warm, bright, and impossible to ignore.

"Hey, team!" Sam's voice cut through the usual pre-meeting lull one morning, buoyant and full of energy. He grinned as if he'd been waiting all week for this exact moment. "Let's make this one for the books, yeah?"

Laughter percolated. Brenda from accounting gave a small eye roll—the affectionate kind. Sam had that rare ability to make even the most skeptical people relax. Somehow, he made work feel a little less like work.

As the discussion got going, he was in his element. Ideas flew, connections formed, people leaned in. *Okay, that landed,* he thought, noticing the corners of Mark's mouth tilt into a rare smile. *Keep it light. Keep it moving.*

Then came the talk of deadlines, budgets, and targets missed. The air grew heavier. Sam felt it in his chest, that familiar gray-rock dip. His knee bounced under the table. *Nope. Not letting this drop.*

Sam leaned forward, his voice bright. "Alright, let's flip this! Honestly, this whole thing could be a goldmine of an opportunity." He smiled, maybe a little too wide, and threw another log on the fire of optimism.

The room loosened. A few people chuckled again. *Crisis averted.* But under the surface, he tensed. *God, I'm running on fumes,* he admitted to himself. *Why does it always feel like it's my job to hold the room together?*

When the meeting finally wrapped, Sam stayed behind, stacking coffee cups, singing under his breath to fill the quiet. His phone buzzed with another invite, another meeting, another chance to keep the energy up. He smiled automatically. *They want you there. Of course they do.*

> **He leaned on the table for a moment, watching a streak of sunlight crawl across it. "Just keep the energy up," he whispered—a promise he'd made to himself too many times before.**

Then, out loud, to no one in particular: "Let's make it fun."

Even the sun has to rise on command sometimes.

How to Recognize The Always-On

The Always-On is the sunshine breaking through on a gray day. They don't just raise the energy in a room; they change it.

They are the live wire that wakes up the meeting that's lost its way, turning small talk into possibility. They have a way of making even the dullest agenda feel like an open dance floor, something to move with, not trudge through.

Their laughter rolls easily, full-bodied and genuine. They don't just tell stories; they pull you into them. Their presence has rhythm and optimism, and you can't deny their quick wit that keeps people anchored. They make you believe that you could actually want to show up for work.

And they do it all with one phrase that feels like both an invitation and a promise:

"Let's make it fun."

It's said not as a throwaway line but as if it were a sacred commandment. For them, fun is oxygen. It's the antidote to monotony, the proof that life, even at work, can feel good. They believe that laughter encourages collaboration, that creativity blooms faster when people are at ease.

Watch closely, though, and you'll see the gears turning beneath the glow. The way their eyes dart around the room, reading expressions before words are spoken. The quick adjustment in tone when someone's mood shifts. They're emotional translators, fluent in the subtle language of group energy. If someone looks tired, they'll brighten their voice. If tension thickens, they'll crack a joke, diffuse the air, and get everyone laughing again.

It's instinct, not calculation. First, they feel the heaviness and hesitation coming from the people around them, and their body responds before their mind catches up. They don't think, *How do I fix this?* Doing so is just instinctual.

When they leave, everyone feels their absence.

That's how you recognize The Always-On; they are the person who carries the beat and keeps the rhythm alive so no one else has to face the silence.

Why The Always-On Is the Way They Are

For The Always-On, joy isn't just an emotion; it's survival.

> *They've built a life around movement, brightness, and connection because stillness has never felt safe.*

In their lives, they've learned that when they shine, people stay. When they bring the energy, things don't fall apart. Maybe it started in childhood, when laughter eased the tension at the dinner table. Maybe it came later, when being the upbeat one was the easiest way to be accepted, admired, or simply included. Whatever the origin, the lesson grew legs early: Keep things light, and you'll be okay.

This belief hardened into instinct. Now, as adults, they move through the world scanning for the tiniest cracks in the mood around them, and they rush to patch them all with optimism. If the vibe feels heavy, they take it personally, as though it's their responsibility to turn the room right side up again.

The Always-On doesn't mean to overextend. It's just that quiet feels like rejection. So, they plug every gap with conversation, laughter, and movement—anything that keeps the energy alive. And though they make it look effortless, it costs them.

The irony is, they give others what they secretly crave for themselves: lightness, ease, belonging. But their own joy often exists on a timer; it's fleeting, borrowed, and conditional based on how much everyone else is smiling.

When they can't find that confirmation, they lose color and become restless and uncertain, then turn to chasing something, anything, that can bring the rhythm back.

For them, invisibility doesn't look like being overlooked. It's being irrelevant. The thought of losing that connection, of no longer being the reason people feel good, is unbearable. So, they keep dazzling, with the music loud enough to drown out the question they can't quite answer: "Who am I when the lights go down?"

The Link

If Sam ever sat down to take a personality test, he'd probably turn it into a group activity. "This is going to be a blast!" he'd crow, spinning his laptop around to compare results with whoever was nearby. And, of course, his chart would light up like a festival, the psychological equivalent of a neon-flashing "OPEN" sign.

In the Enneagram, The Always-On is mostly a blend of Type 7, The Enthusiast, with Type 4, The Individualist, complementing the mix. The 7 explains the endless curiosity, the need to keep life sunny, the refusal to be pinned down by boredom or pain. Type 4 adds the emotional depth, that craving for meaning behind the laughter, the desire to be unique, authentic, and unforgettable. Together, these types create a personality that radiates possibility while the person in the driver's seat secretly wonders if they're too much or not enough, all at once.

The Big Five paints a similar picture: high Extraversion, high Openness. These people are the connectors, the storytellers, the ones who turn routine into rhythm. They find joy in the unknown, fuel in interaction, and meaning in momentum. But when the world slows down, when there's no one to bounce off, their thoughts can echo too loudly.

On the DiSC profile, The Always-On lives squarely in I: Influence. Charismatic, spontaneous, and people-focused, they thrive on movement and recognition. They can rally a team faster than most can finish a sentence, but they often mistake harmony for happiness. When energy flags, they obliterate the silence before it eats them alive.

And if you look at their CliftonStrengths, you'll see words that read almost like a playlist of their soul: Communication, Activator, Ideation, Command, Self-Assurance, Significance, Input, Arranger, and Woo. The Always-On is built for momentum with their contagious strength and magnetic enthusiasm.

They bring lightness, forward motion, and possibility into every room they enter, but that same energy can be disorienting for others. Conversations can stay buoyant even when something heavier wants to be named. Moments that ask for stillness are quickly lifted with humor, optimism, or a reassuring "It's not that bad."

People may feel energized around Sam, yet be unsure whether there's space to slow down or be fully heard.

And for Sam, always being the one who lifts the room eventually becomes exhausting. Like any great song played too loudly for too long, what makes them extraordinary can begin to distort. The very qualities that keep everything moving are often the ones quietly draining them.

Across every model, the theme is the same: The Always-On is wired for joy and connection and terrified of losing it.

How to Work Alongside The Always-On

If you've got an Always-On on your team, you already know the difference they make. Meetings run more smoothly, ideas flow more easily, and even hard days feel a little lighter when they're around. They have this rare ability to turn "just another workday" into an invigorating entity. They're the bridge between the quiet thinkers and the loud ones, moving people from "stuck" to eager.

Here's the part that's easy to miss: Their brightness is not infinite. It's borrowed light, drawn from somewhere deep inside, and if you never look beneath the luster, you'll miss the fatigue hiding there.

They'll never tell you that they're running low, not because they don't trust you, but because they've built an identity around being the person who always has more to give. They equate joy with usefulness. They believe that if they're not lifting the room, they're literally letting it down.

> **So, if you want to work well with them, don't just enjoy their energy; protect it.**

Watch how they operate. They're often the ones suggesting the next idea, proposing something bigger, or injecting fresh energy when things start to feel flat. They bring movement into moments that might otherwise stall, not because they're asked to, but because it feels natural to keep things going.

If you slow the moment down and ask how that constant momentum is actually landing for them, you create something rare: permission to pause. A brief space to stop performing and notice what it costs to always be the spark.

Check in with them beyond the surface. Not the polite, "How are you?" that triggers them to spit out a bubbly answer, but a question probing, "You don't have to make this fun; how are you *really*?"

Permit them to have off days. To take some self-care time and not be the spark. If you're their leader, model that quieter persona yourself. Show them that reflectiveness isn't failure; it's recovery (and it's necessary). If you're their teammate, don't just take their sunshine; offer shade and your own rays of light. Sometimes the kindest thing you can do for an Always-On is let them sit in silence and feel what it's like not to mistake chatter for security.

When they do slow down and finally let their mask slip, revealing exhaustion, don't rush to reassure them. Don't say, "But you're always so positive!" Try, "You don't have to be positive today."

That's how you work alongside The Always-On.

Not by matching their energy, but by joining in the effort to encourage and build up your fellow teammates—giving them a break and a wake-up call that when their energy slows, they are still valuable.

What If You Are The Always-On?

If, as you were reading this, you recognized you've spent a lifetime being the light for others, I got you.

You and I both know that behind every spark is a glimmer of exhaustion. You've learned to shine through the cracks, to keep smiling even when the glow feels forced.

You tell yourself you're fine, that this is who you are, that maybe other people just aren't wired to bring the light. But deep down, you know the truth: Even the sun gets tired of rising on command.

But here's what's truer than that fear of reducing your wattage: You are not loved for your light. You are loved for your depth. Not because you're always upbeat or inspiring, but because of who you are when the energy drops, when the jokes stop, when things feel heavy or uncertain. You don't have to earn your belonging by keeping everyone else happy. You don't have to outrun stillness to matter. The people who truly care about you don't just want your brightness; they want *all* of you, including the quiet, tired, complicated parts.

You are allowed to be real and feel real emotions, even if they are troubling, and you need to learn to work through them.

You are allowed to pause and hear the silence.

You are allowed to take a breath and not fill the space immediately after it.

Start by saying less. Notice the next time you feel the urge to lift the energy, to throw yourself into the gap, to smooth the silence, then pause, even for three seconds. Let it be uncomfortable if it has to be. It won't always be this way. Believe it or not, you can even get used to a pregnant pause. Most importantly, remind yourself: You don't owe the world your constant spark.

Joy doesn't vanish when you rest. It changes shape into less obtrusive, consistent contentment that satiates you, not just everyone else.

Your Next Step

If this chapter feels like the sunlight you didn't know you needed, don't stop here. Awareness is powerful, but practice is next-level. Take the free Invisible Work Archetype Assessment to see which patterns are running your workday, and join **The 7-Day Archetype Reset Challenge**, involving simple, daily prompts designed to help you rediscover joy that doesn't depend on being "on."

Start your reset at ChooseYouBook.com.

You've spent your life keeping the room alive.

Now it's your turn to feel alive in it.

Chapter 12:

The Hurricane

"So What"
—P!nk

Vicky didn't need theatrics to command attention. When she asked who had approved the latest version of the project materials, her voice was steady and deliberate, the kind that made people straighten without quite knowing why. The room didn't freeze; it recalibrated. Chairs shifted. Screens were adjusted. Everyone understood that this wasn't a question designed for discussion.

She stepped closer to the screen and pointed. The numbers didn't hold. The assumptions were loose. The language was vague in places where leadership would expect precision. She spoke clearly, moving from issue to issue without softening the edges. "This doesn't line up with the projections," she said. "And this section reads like no one wanted to commit to a position." Then, almost as an aside, "There's also a typo in the header. After three reviews."

Her feedback was specific and unsentimental. "This isn't your best work," she said, matter-of-factly. "And I won't put my name on something like this." She wasn't trying to embarrass anyone. She was trying to keep unfinished, careless work from leaving the room. *This is how things unravel,* she thought. *Not through big failures, but through small tolerances.*

Vicky laid out what needed to happen next, outlining a revised forecast, clear ownership for each section, and a tighter rollout plan. She didn't present any of it as optional, because in her mind it wasn't. This work would go straight to senior leadership, and it would carry her name with it. *If this lands badly, it lands on me,* she thought, steady and unsentimental. *And I don't miss.*

When someone muttered something about workload, Vicky turned toward the sound. "Workload?" she repeated, keeping her voice level. "I'm not asking for more. I'm asking for better."

She meant it. To her, pressure didn't create problems; it exposed them. If someone struggled under the pace, that struggle wasn't new. It had just been hidden by time, comfort, or lowered expectations. Better to see it now than be surprised later, when the stakes were higher and the audience less forgiving.

Vicky organized work in short, intense sprints, setting tight deadlines and expecting people to move with purpose. She watched carefully, not just for results but for reactions. *Who stayed focused when things sped up? Who needed constant reassurance? Who lost their footing the moment decisions had to be made without a safety net? I need to know who I can rely on,* she thought. *I can't afford to be caught off guard.*

People sought her out because she was smart, composed, and decisive. She saw gaps others missed and named them without hesitation. At the same time, they learned to brace themselves before speaking to her. Feedback came fast and direct, stripped of cushioning. Vicky believed clarity was a form of respect. Sugarcoating felt dishonest to her, even irresponsible. If the work wasn't strong enough, she said so.

Underneath that certainty lived a belief she rarely questioned but always acted on: *If I don't stay on top of this, someone else will.* Control wasn't about ego. It was about safety.

Staying ahead meant no one could corner her, undermine her, or rewrite the story without her knowing. Letting go felt risky.

Someone else's grip could tighten quickly, and she had learned early how hard it was to get leverage back once it slipped away.

When she told herself she was helping, she believed it. High standards made people sharper. Honest feedback made them better. What she didn't always see was how often that constant pressure taught people to protect themselves around her. They didn't grow more confident; they grew more careful.

Vicky wasn't trying to be liked. She wasn't chasing praise or trying to prove her worth. That wasn't what drove her. She wanted authority over the work and influence over how decisions were made. Control meant she didn't have to wait and see what happened next. As long as she stayed ahead of the moment, she didn't have to find out what it felt like to be overtaken.

How to Recognize The Hurricane

You'll know a Hurricane the moment you cross their orbit. The room puckers when they arrive. Conversations shorten. People think a little harder and choose their words more carefully. It's not fear exactly, but awareness. Everyone understands that whatever is said next will be examined closely.

Her presence brings speed and pressure. Ideas don't drift casually when she's involved. They are tested. Turned. Questioned from every angle until only the strongest version remains, or until the person presenting them begins to doubt whether they were ready to speak at all. To The Hurricane, challenge isn't personal. It's necessary. Weak thinking feels dangerous, and she has no patience for it.

You'll hear her ask questions that sound reasonable on the surface but are actually weighty. She wants to know the logic, the risk, the upside, the downside, and why the group is still talking instead of moving.

> *Her curiosity is not exploratory; it's evaluative. She listens for gaps, not possibilities. What she calls "exceptional" is work that leaves no room for surprise, no loose ends, no one else in a position to challenge her later.*

People often mistake her intensity for mentorship. She is smart, put together, and decisive. When she points out flaws, it can feel, in retrospect, like she was trying to help. And sometimes she is. But the deeper driver isn't the development of others. It's the need to ensure nothing slips past her control. If someone rises, that's fine. If someone fails, that's acceptable, too. What matters is that the outcome never threatens *her* standing.

Her delivery lacks softness because softness feels risky. Praise comes rarely, and only when it reinforces authority rather than generosity.

When she leaves the room, the energy shifts. People breathe again. The pace slows. There's relief, but also uncertainty, as if the scaffolding she provided has been removed along with the pressure. The air feels calmer but less defined.

To her, challenge is love in disguise. Regardless of her stainless-steel appeal, she pulls people into motion. That's how you recognize The Hurricane: They are the ones shaking up the system, not out of rebellion, but out of the belief that everyone and everything can be stronger than they are right now.

Why Hurricanes Are the Way They Are

Vicky didn't decide to become The Hurricane. Her sharpness and relentless drive didn't come from ambition alone. They came from learning early on that certainty kept her safe. Being right meant staying upright. Being decisive meant staying in the room. Doubt, hesitation, or asking for help felt like invitations for someone else to step in and take over.

That lesson may have arrived early in environments where confidence was rewarded, and second-guessing was corrected quickly. Or it may have come later in workplaces where visibility belonged to the loudest voices, and mistakes stuck longer than successes. Wherever it began, the message was clear: Power protects. Vicky absorbed that truth and built herself accordingly. She became someone who could not be overlooked, ignored, or easily challenged.

When things go wrong, she doesn't soften or retreat. She buckles down. If someone misses a detail, that confirms what she already suspected. If a plan wobbles, it reinforces her belief that vigilance is non-negotiable. She isn't looking for reasons to be upset. She genuinely believes there is always more to refine, more to secure, more to lock down before something breaks.

Every question she asks, every standard she enforces, every structure she insists on serves the same purpose: keeping chaos at bay. Pushing people past comfort isn't cruelty in her mind. It's preparation.

What she doesn't see is how this lands. She assumes people respect her intensity. She believes they look up to her, even when they fall quiet around her. Fear doesn't register as fear. It reads as seriousness. Compliance feels like alignment. Her need to protect herself leaves little room to question whether her presence feels safe to others.

The cost of this way of operating is high, though she rarely names it. Carrying the weight of every outcome, every decision, every potential failure leaves her tired in ways she doesn't quite understand.

On rare occasions, she feels a longing for ease, for the relief of trusting that things might hold together without her constant grip. But that thought passes quickly. Letting go is reckless.

So, she sharpens her tone again and carries on, mistaking control for safety once more because, for most of her life, they have felt like the same thing.

The Link

If you mapped Vicky across different behavioral frameworks, you'd see the same shape appear again and again, drawn in different ink. Clear lines. Defined edges. Very little gray space. Control, confidence, conviction. These traits built her career and carried her into positions of influence. They are also the traits that quietly wear on her when no one is paying attention.

In Enneagram terms, she sits firmly in Type 8, The Challenger. The protector who moves first, takes charge, and relies on certainty to stay grounded. At her best, this energy is powerful. She steps into situations others avoid, makes decisions under pressure, and brings structure where there is confusion. In its shadow, that same instinct to control becomes more rigid. The influence of Type 1, The Reformer, shows up here, too, pulling her toward precision, structure, and a strong sense of what is right. It's not enough for her to succeed. She needs to succeed on *her* terms.

Through the Big Five lens, she would likely register low in Agreeableness, not because she lacks care, but because she prioritizes truth over tact. She is also sky-high in assertiveness and Conscientiousness. Politeness can feel inefficient to her. When others hesitate, she steps in because action feels safer than uncertainty. That instinct keeps things moving, and it also creates distance she rarely notices.

DiSC places her clearly in the Dominance category. She is direct, decisive, and allergic to hesitation. In her world, clarity equals competence. Give her a target, and she will find a way to hit it or remove whatever stands in the way. When pushed too far, that same dominance can take up all the space in a room, leaving little room for discussion and a lot of room for direction.

Her CliftonStrengths tell the same story in another language. Command. Competition. Self-Assurance. Analytical. Significance. Belief. Focus. Discipline. These are the fingerprints of her brilliance. They allow her to see the potential in broken systems and give her the nerve to rebuild them.

When overextended, she burns through inefficiency quickly and empathy quietly.

Across all these models, the pattern holds. Vicky has been conditioned to take charge as a way of staying safe. None of these traits is inherently bad. It's their combination that makes her formidable. What she rarely allows herself to do is turn that same precision inward and ask a harder question. Not *What needs fixing?* Or *Who needs to step up?* But *What am I protecting myself from if I stop pushing?* She doesn't avoid this question out of denial, but out of instinct, because slowing down enough to hear the answer feels far riskier than continuing as she is.

How to Work Alongside The Hurricane

Working with someone like Vicky can feel a little like standing near an electric fence. There's energy, brilliance, and forward motion, but if you're not grounded, you'll feel the jolt.

She'll challenge you, question you, and occasionally bulldoze your ideas in the name of progress—without noticing you're standing in a pile of charred rubble. But here's the secret: Beneath that intensity isn't arrogance, it's responsibility. To her, high standards are acts of care, even if they don't sound that way in the moment.

So how do you work with someone who's built like a storm and powered by principle?

First, don't mistake her confidence for invincibility. Vicky respects strength, not bravado; she prizes steadiness, not fits and starts. If you disagree with her, do it clearly and calmly. She doesn't trust flattery, but she does trust facts. Bring data, not drama. When she asks hard questions, answer them directly. Vagueness reads as incompetence.

Second, set boundaries early and keep them. She pushes because she assumes everyone's capacity matches her own. It's not malicious; it's habit. She literally can't tap into reasons for defensiveness or hurt. When you say no, she might test it. Hold your line anyway. You'll earn her respect faster than if you fold.

Third, give her outcomes, not updates. She doesn't want to wade through process details. Show her progress, and she'll back off. Miss a deadline without warning, though, and she'll double her oversight in a heartbeat.

And finally, acknowledge her strength sincerely. Tell her when her precision saved the team or when her push got results. Praise to Vicky isn't about ego. It's about trust. It tells her she can step back without the whole thing collapsing.

If you can learn to see past the hard shell she's built around herself, you'll notice something unexpected: Vicky's not trying to dominate the room; she's trying to keep it intact. The best way to work with her isn't to douse her fire; it's to ground it. When the team consistently meets her standards without being pushed, it's evidence that she doesn't have to hold everything together by herself.

What If You Are The Hurricane?

If you were reading this and felt your shoulders bunch up, that's okay. You've spent so long bracing yourself against chaos that you've forgotten what it feels like to unclench.

You built this strength for a reason. Somewhere along the way, you learned that certainty keeps you safe, that leadership means control, and that people respect you more when you're unshakable. And maybe they do. But respect built on fear is a lonely kind of power.

You don't have to be the sharpest voice in the room to be heard. The people who truly value you aren't looking for perfection; they're looking for presence.

When you are ready to make a change, start small. If someone offers help, accept it without apology. If things don't go exactly to plan, resist the urge to clamp down harder. Let something be *good enough* without sprinting to fix it. You might be surprised at how many outcomes hold up without your constant vigilance.

If you've spent your whole life building armor, please know this: It doesn't make you unlovable; it just means you've been protecting that vulnerable part of you that longs to trust others without the fear of being let down.

Power doesn't always come from being the loudest, the strongest, or the most precise. Sometimes, real power shows up in decisions others don't even know about. Allowing someone else to take the lead or stepping back without scanning for what might go wrong is empowering. The world doesn't fall apart when you relax, but you may finally notice how much effort it's taken to keep all the pieces together.

You've already proven you can carry more than most. What you may not have noticed is the cost of doing it alone. When you're constantly on alert for what might slip, you don't just wear others down; you wear yourself thin.

Delegation isn't a loss of power; it's a release of the pressure you've been absorbing for years.

Learning to trust others isn't about lowering your standards. It's about realizing that strength doesn't have to be proven through endurance and that you don't need to break yourself to stay standing.

Your Next Step

If you can relate to this chapter, take it as data, not as a defect in your character. You don't need to overhaul who you are; you just need to give that strength a healthier outlet. Mentor young talent, start a passion project, or volunteer at a local charity, for instance.

Take the free Invisible Work Archetype Assessment to see which pattern drives your leadership style, which will lead you into **The 7-Day Archetype Reset Challenge**, designed with short, practical prompts to help you release control without losing your edge.

Start your reset at ChooseYouBook.com.

Because you don't have to earn respect through relentless control, you already have it.

Chapter 13:

The Magnet

"Fast Car"
—Tracy Chapman

The new job. Ah, the glorious, shiny new job. Jonas had appreciated that fresh-paint, crisp-linen smell for exactly 11 days, 11 full days of optimism, of early alarms and ironed shirts, of almost believing this time would be different. This time, maybe the boss would actually know what they were doing. The team would take responsibility. The jokes would stop when it was time to work.

Jonas had learned not to name this hope out loud. Seven jobs in nine years had taught him that somehow, without trying, he had a talent for landing in the same place wearing different logos. An incompetent boss who failed upward. A team drifting on laissez-faire attitudes. It was as if dysfunction could spot him across a crowded LinkedIn feed.

And then came day 12.

Jonas sat in the conference room that always smelled faintly of reheated leftovers and whiteboard markers, a scent he privately called "corporate despair."

Someone kept clicking their pen. *Click. Click. Click.* He could practically feel his sanity splintering with each staccato sound. *Is this a meeting or a test of endurance?* he thought, pressing his tongue against the back of his teeth to stop himself from sighing.

Across the table, his manager smiled. Bright, composed, every hair in place, she said, "Let's talk about realigning priorities."

Jonas didn't look up, but the words hit anyway. "Realigning." *Corporate speak for someone messed up, and we're about to find out who. Priorities. Code for more work, less sleep. No thanks.* He could already feel his pulse quickening, that familiar knot forming in his stomach. *Here we go. Another round of Blame Bingo.*

Jonas let his eyes rest on the spreadsheet in front of him, the blue grid blurring slightly. Numbers were safe. Numbers never asked follow-up questions.

"Jonas," his manager said, pleasant as ever.

His stomach dropped. *Of course. Always me. Always day 12.*

He looked up, managing a half-smile that felt like cardboard. "Yeah?"

"What's your read on the rollout delays? I'd love your take before we finalize next steps."

Her tone was genuinely kind, but Jonas didn't buy it. He never did. *Ah, there it is,* he thought. *The velvet hammer. Ask nicely; accuse quietly. Works every time.*

He straightened in his chair, tugging at his tie. "Well … I think some of the initial expectations might not have been as clear as they could've been." The sentence came out measured, diplomatic, the verbal equivalent of tiptoeing through a minefield.

Her brow creased slightly, not in criticism but curiosity. "Okay. What would've made it clearer?"

Jonas blinked. *Trap question. That same trap question.* He could feel everyone watching now, even though no one was. "Just … better communication maybe," he offered, his voice a shade too soft.

"Alright," she said simply, nodding. "Let's make sure we build that in next time."

> **And that was it. She moved on. The world didn't implode, the sky didn't fall, yet Jonas' heart was still recovering from the shot of adrenaline. It didn't matter what anyone else heard; he always left these moments feeling smaller, less lively.**

As the meeting wrapped, chairs scraped back, and laughter rippled from the corner, easy, unbothered patter that made Jonas' jaw clench. He lingered behind, not quite ready to rejoin the current of bodies flowing toward the door. Instead, he stepped to the window. The river slid past below, like those bodies, steady and unconcerned, carrying everything along without pause or permission. Jonas watched it move, feeling the familiar weight settle in his chest. Nothing he said here would change its direction. Some things just kept going, whether he was ready or not.

Jonas listened to the others talk about happy hour, about their lives that apparently existed beyond these walls.

Must be nice, he thought. Some people get to clock out of this place. I just take it home with me in a to-go box of anxiety.

After enough punishment, he finally stood, shrugging on his jacket. Outside the window, the river had shifted color; it was darker now, thicker with shadow. It marked time better than any clock. Workday over, current unchanged.

It's just bad leadership, he murmured, letting the words settle over him like a comforting blanket.

It was his refrain, his ritual, his quiet way of explaining everything that hurt without ever looking too closely at why it hurt so much.

He paused at the door, glancing back at the empty table, the battlefield of coffee cups, abandoned pens, and half-scribbled notes. "We're like a family," they'd said in the interview, with that corporate "earnestness" that had sounded so warm at the time. Except this was the kind of family where the dad forgets your birthday, the mom helicopters your every move, and your older sibling steals your Halloween candy, yet somehow you're the one who apologizes for not buying more.

Jonas shook his head. *They'll never change,* he thought. *Places like this, people like that ... they just don't.* Day 12 was the end of the line. The optimism had disintegrated, and reality dawned.

Jonas stepped into the hallway, the electric buzz of the office folding around him again, making him feel that he was always just a little too underprepared—under-something—for the life he still secretly hoped might be waiting for him.

How to Recognize The Magnet

You'll spot a Magnet by what they don't say. They're the ones whose body language tells a different story than their words—they'll nod along while their arms stay crossed and agree in the moment, but sigh just loud enough to be heard as they walk away.

They show up, do their work, and keep their head down. They're not difficult. They're compliant. But beneath that steadiness runs a current of bristling judgment. The boss doesn't know what they're doing. The team doesn't pull its weight. The strategy won't work, but no one asked them, so *Why bother saying anything?*

When things go wrong—and they're already expecting them to—you won't hear them take ownership. Instead, you'll hear the passive voice do all the heavy lifting. "The timeline wasn't realistic." "Communication could have been better." "Expectations weren't clear." They're not wrong, exactly. But they're also *never* responsible.

> **Their questions aren't challenges; they're insurance policies. "What if the timeline slips?" "Have we thought about what happens when ...?" "I'm not sure the team is ready for that."**

It sounds like prudence, and sometimes it is. But more often, it's a way of voicing concern without having to propose a solution—or be accountable if it all goes sideways.

You'll rarely see them volunteer for the messy, visible work. They're too smart for that. *Why stick your neck out when leadership will just change direction next week? Why invest when the odds are already stacked against success?* They're not lazy; they're diplomatic. At least, that's how *they* see it.

The Magnet believes they're the dependable one, the steady force keeping the team or project on point while chaos swirls around them. And in some ways, they are. They show up on time. They meet deadlines. They don't make waves. But they also don't make moves. They wait for the environment to prove itself—and it never does.

Here's the tell: Ask them about their last three jobs, and you'll hear the same story in different settings. Incompetent leadership. Unclear priorities. A team that didn't take things seriously. After the third retelling, you'll start to notice the pattern. It's always someone else's fault, and they're always the one who saw it coming.

They don't storm out or make a scene. They just stop believing you, and that distance becomes their new default. The commitment they once had—the quiet dependability you thought you could count on—evaporates without announcement. They're still there, technically. But the part of them that cared has already left the building.

That's how you recognize The Magnet: They're the ones convinced they keep landing in the same broken situations, never quite connecting that they might be drawing them in.

Why Magnets Are the Way They Are

Jonas didn't wake up one day and decide to see the world through monotone-tinted glasses. The glass half empty, the sigh before the sentence, the quiet conviction that nothing ever really works out; those weren't choices. They were learned habits.

People don't start out expecting disappointment; they are taught that anticipating it minimizes the hits. Sometimes they learn this through life, and sometimes from people who loved them but didn't know how to show it. Maybe Jonas grew up in a house where the volume was always a little too loud, where mistakes were pointed out before wins were celebrated, where "Nice effort" was the closest thing to praise. Or maybe it wasn't as obvious as that. Maybe his parents overcorrected every fall, stepping in so fast that he never got the chance to see what standing back up on his own two feet felt like.

That kind of love, the anxious, overprotective kind, can leave a child safe but untested. And when you grow up without the small triumphs of fixing what's broken or trying and failing and trying again, the world starts to feel like a place that happens *to* you, not *for* you.

> **So, Jonas learned early that control was fragile. That if something went wrong, it was safer to blame the storm than admit he might've been holding the umbrella upside down.**

It was safer to assume the worst, that people would disappoint him, that leaders couldn't be trusted, that every "new beginning" was just the prequel to another ending.

He tells himself it's realism. That he's not negative, just prepared, but what he's really doing is pre-rejecting life before it has the chance to reject him. That's what his cynicism protects: dangerous hope. Hoping means he could be wrong again. And Jonas would rather feel certain in his disappointment than risk being surprised by it and unsure what to do about it.

When someone in authority challenges him, even kindly, he hears accusation. When a colleague offers feedback, he interprets it as betrayal. He's not dramatic about it; he just shores up his guard without ruffling any collars, rehearses his defense, and retreats into the comfortable certainty that it's all out of his hands anyway. "Bad leadership," he mutters; it's the truth that keeps him warm.

But that warmth is a trap, a slow burn that numbs instead of heals. It keeps him safe, yes, but stunts his growth. Because underneath all the rationalizations and recycled frustrations, Jonas isn't lazy or bitter; he's scared. Scared that if he stopped blaming the system, he might have to confront how much power he actually has.

And the idea of possessing power to someone who's only known it as something used *against* them is scary to the point of self-sabotage. Not because they see power as an option and reject it, but because they've been holding the umbrella upside down for so long, it hasn't even occurred to them that it could be turned the other way.

> *It's better to stay where it's familiar, in that uneasy middle ground between safety and resignation, waiting for the world to change while quietly bracing for it not to.*

The Link

If The Pleaser chases harmony and The Always-On feeds on connection, The Magnet craves a security that makes life predictable, contained, and controllable. Their deepest need is to feel supported and prepared for whatever might go wrong, and their greatest fear is being blindsided. For Jonas, that means scanning constantly for risk and disappointment, reading the room before it speaks, and lowering expectations before they can hurt him. Over time, that vigilance starts to shape where he ends up. When every environment is approached as something likely to fail, it's easier to notice incompetence everywhere else.

In Enneagram terms, The Magnet reflects The Loyalist, Type 6. They try to be devoted to the people and systems they want to trust, but are on constant alert for the moment that trust might break. They don't challenge the ground beneath them; they quietly adapt to its cracks, assuming instability is inevitable. It can feel safer to brace themselves and comply than to take a step that might actually change the terrain.

> **By staying quiet, adapting quickly, and letting decisions be made around them, they trade short-term comfort for long-term frustration.**

The irony is that their need for stability often creates the very turbulence they're trying to avoid.

On the DiSC profile, they sit squarely in the S quadrant—Steadiness; they are just that, as well as loyal and quietly dependable.

And in CliftonStrengths language, The Magnet's gifts read like a safety manual: Responsibility, Consistency, Context, Belief, Deliberative, Connectedness, Intellection. Each quality is a beautiful expression of loyalty, reflection, and foresight, but when pushed too far, they can recast possibility as something dangerous rather than inviting.

That's what makes The Magnet both indispensable and misunderstood. Their radar for what could go wrong is unmatched: catching weaknesses early, spotting misalignment before it turns public, and asking the questions others skip until it's too late. But that same radar is tuned so high that it sometimes mistakes curiosity for threat. Where others see a blank slate, Jonas sees a potential mess. Where others see a challenge, he sees the chance to fail in public. As a result, he stays shut down, not because he lacks courage, but because he's exhausted from always being alert.

The thing about Magnets is that their steady predictability and cautious preparation attract the very outcomes they're trying to defend against. They hold back effort because they're certain it won't be recognized, approach leadership with quiet contempt disguised as compliance, and keep their emotional armor so locked down that others learn not to lean in. Over time, that distance reads as disengagement, that defensiveness as fragility, and the promotion they never truly reached for goes to someone louder, less prepared, but easier to back. It's not sabotage; it's survival. If they expect disappointment, they can't be surprised by it, and that feels so much safer. Lather, rinse, repeat.

If you're the one who walks into new jobs, expecting the worst, know this: You're not unlucky. You're not doomed to keep landing in the same storms. You've just spent so long preparing for the worst that you've forgotten what it feels like when things actually go right. Maybe take a moment to recall a time when you had a good day or experience to test your mind and genuine recall.

> ***Not every lull is the calm before disaster. Sometimes the river slows, the surface smooths, and nothing demands your attention at all. And it's okay to stand there without scanning the current for what might pull you under.***

How to Work Alongside The Magnet

Working with someone like Jonas requires patience, not the sigh-and-endure kind, but that constancy that builds trust brick by brick. Magnets like him don't resist leadership out of defiance; they're not difficult, they're careful.

If you lead or partner with a Magnet, consistency is your currency. Involve them early, make the process visible, and let change arrive through explanation rather than surprise. Don't shock them with last-minute pivots and call it "agility." To them, unpredictability isn't exciting; it's unsafe. When you can, show your work. Let them see the why behind a decision. It won't just earn their cooperation; it will earn their confidence, and maybe, just maybe, it will move them from second-guessing to full belief.

Magnets thrive under leaders who keep their word, follow through, and don't weaponize mistakes. Accountability is fine; public correction is not. The fastest way to lose a Magnet's trust is to embarrass them. The fastest way to gain it is to stay calm when things go wrong and normalize that mistakes happen.

Ask for their input early, but not as an afterthought. They're at their best when they feel part of the process, not startled by the outcome. They'll likely begin with hesitation: "*Are you sure you want my opinion?*" Keep inviting them anyway. Over time, those small invitations become proof that their voice is safe to use—and that you want to hear it. This is what they want most—empirical evidence that they are needed, that their ideas can advance an agenda.

When they get stuck in "*what-if*" loops, don't rush to fix them. These spirals aren't complacency; they're anxiety trying to prevent pain before it arrives. Gently redirect and ask, "And what if it goes right?" This question won't solve everything, but it opens a window where a wall used to be.

Above all, don't mistake their skepticism for cynicism. They're not trying to sink the ship; they're trying to make sure there are enough lifeboats. *I want this to go well,* Jonas thinks. *I just don't think it's going to.* Their worry is their loyalty in disguise.

What If You Are The Magnet?

If this chapter resonated, take a well-earned, cleansing, anxiety-chasing breath. You've spent a lifetime preparing for disappointment, and you don't need to lower your guard all at once. When a colleague offers help, resist the reflex to wonder what it will cost. Thank them, and let it stand. When something goes right, don't rush to find the catch and throw yourself into a well-worn pattern of chaos-familiarity. Let yourself have the moment.

You want the truth? Life doesn't have to feel this hard or carry this much weight. You've built a world where struggle feels like proof that you're trying, but it's okay for it to be easier. It's okay for people to show up for you without you needing to earn it.

Your Next Step

If you saw yourself in Jonas, forever waiting for the next storm, don't stop here. Awareness is the first step toward change, but it's the small daily shifts that build the real safety you've been chasing.

Take the free Invisible Work Archetype Assessment to uncover your patterns at work, and automatically join **The 7-Day Archetype Reset Challenge**. Seven gentle prompts can help you stop steeling yourself and start believing again.

Start your reset at ChooseYouBook.com.

Chapter 14:

The Placeholder

"Wake Me Up"
—Avicii

Renee's keyboard was older than her nephew. She knew this because she'd been at the company longer than her nephew had been alive, 21 years, 15 of them in the same role, at the same desk, with the same view of the same crooked tree outside the same window. She could tell the seasons not by the weather but by that tree: leaves pushing out unevenly in spring, a full, overreaching canopy by summer, and in winter, branches stripped back to bare bark against the glass.

The morning started like every other: the familiar chime of the elevator, the soft shuffle of shoes down the hall, and the hiss of the new coffee machine churning out someone's vanilla latte. The scent drifted through the office, mingling with the faint aroma of printer toner and the lemon wipes Renee kept neatly stowed in her drawer beside her emergency chocolate stash.

"Hey, Renee?" a voice called from across the cubicle divide. It was Eric, one of the newer hires, all energy and optimism, the kind of *Always-On* enthusiasm that still believed "urgent" emails could change the world. "Do you know if the regional team's flights have been booked for next week?"

Without looking up, Renee smiled. "Already done. I know, I know, I didn't have to, but I saw the email come through and figured I'd handle it. Upgraded seats confirmed, transfers arranged, and the hotel moved to one with decent Wi-Fi. They'll thank you for it later."

Eric was effusive. "*You're amazing. Seriously, what would we do without you?*"

That question, *What would we do without you,* landed exactly where Renee liked it, offering little warmth but just enough validation to remind her that she mattered. She loved being the quiet problem-solver, the one who knew the hidden codes, the person who could make chaos look effortless. Being needed made her feel safe.

Her fingers hovered over the keyboard, hesitating before sending one more confirmation email she'd already checked twice. Maybe she'd read it once more, just to be sure. Maybe she'd go ahead and pre-book the next trip, even though the request hadn't come through yet. It was easier to stay ahead than risk falling behind.

"Renee, you ever thought about applying for that operations lead role? You basically run things anyway." Eric again, bless him. She chuckled softly, deflecting without inviting further curiosity. "Oh no, I'm fine right here. I like what I do."

> **"Fine." It was her favorite word. Reliable, neutral, safe.**
> **"Fine" meant no surprises and no risk. "Fine" meant she'd never have to start over.**

Renee liked getting in early to beat the traffic, but really, she liked getting there before anyone else had a claim on the day. She moved through the office, turning on lights that no one had asked her to touch, opening the blinds one by one, letting morning settle in properly. In the break room, she started the coffee maker, measuring grounds by instinct, not instructions.

Someone has to do it, she thought, rinsing the spoon. *Might as well be me.* She paused, just briefly, wondering if anyone even knew who made the coffee. The thought surfaced and passed.

At her desk, she opened her inbox, not because anything was waiting, but because it needed to be clear. Messages filed. Follow-ups noted. Order restored before the day had a chance to complicate it. Only then did she sit back, jacket folded neatly over the chair, bag tucked beneath the desk.

And the workday hadn't even started yet.

Instead, she opened the company's travel calendar again, scrolling through future trips she'd already planned. There was nothing new to add, nothing to fix, but her fingers still moved, tapping lightly, keeping the rhythm of habit alive. It wasn't urgency. It was familiarity. The illusion of motion in a life that hadn't moved in years.

She glanced at the tree outside, that same, faithful stalwart she'd been watching for just over two decades. The branches trembled in the early morning breeze. For a moment, Renee wondered what it would feel like to let go of the ground she'd been standing on for so long, to lean the other way, even just a little.

"Pfft! I'm fine," she whispered, reaching for her cup of coffee. "Really."

Outside, the sky had lightened to a soft pink-orange. The tree swayed gently, steady against the wind. And for the first time in a long time, Renee noticed that it wasn't standing perfectly still; it bent, stretched, and moved, yet it never fell.

Her 20-year service award caught the light as she shifted, the glass reflecting her face back at her, slightly distorted. She held it there for a moment longer than necessary.

"Maybe," she whispered, barely audible, "it's time to see what else the wind feels like." Renee took a sip, knowing that she'd never do anything of the sort.

The elevator chimed somewhere down the hall as the day officially began. Outside, the tree bent with the breeze before resuming its usual stance. And Renee, dependable, cautious, quietly brilliant Renee, stayed exactly where she was.

How to Recognize The Placeholder

You'll know The Placeholder, though it might take a while. Not because they fade into the background, but because everything works so smoothly when they're around that no one stops to ask why. You're far more likely to recognize them when they're not there, when deadlines pass, details are missed, and the question circulates quietly: *Who usually handles this?*

If you've ever worked with someone who knows *everything*, the history of every project, the passwords no one wrote down, the reason behind every odd process, you've met a Placeholder. They are the keepers of institutional memory, the ones who can tell you what happened in 2011 and why "We don't do it that way anymore." They can find anything, fix anything, and somehow make it all look effortless.

Their desk is neat but personal: a few family photos, maybe a little plant that's been half-alive for years, and a coffee mug that's seen every era of the company logo. They're not loud, but they're essential. And they like it that way. Being needed feels better than being visible.

Renee doesn't chase the spotlight. She holds the system together from the sidelines. She's the one you call when you need something done *right* because she'll do it faster, better, and with less drama than anyone else. Ask her how she's doing, and you'll almost always get the same answer: "I'm fine, really." Her superiors love that about her and heap on increasing responsibility, which she accepts graciously, knowing somewhere in the back of her mind that they don't care about her burdens as long as everything keeps running.

She has made a career out of making work easier for everyone else.

The Placeholder is the calm in the storm, but she's also the reason nothing ever changes. Everything she's worked on has been designed to rely on her. Her comfort zone isn't just cozy, it's reinforced. She knows that if she just keeps everything running smoothly, she'll never have to face the uncertainty of "what's next." She's not lazy, far from it, but she's careful. The kind of careful that confuses peace with avoidance.

You might notice her instinctively stepping back from new opportunities amidst polite excuses. "That's not really my area." "I'm happy to support whoever takes the lead." "I'm good where I am."

If a new system rolls out, she'll learn it but not love it. She'll adapt because she has to, not because she wants to. And when someone younger, louder, or bolder gets promoted past her, she'll clap genuinely, then retreat to her desk, telling herself she never wanted that accolade anyway.

Still, a sadness rims her steadiness. It's the sound of potential and brilliance unspent.

So, when you hear her say, "*I'm fine, really,*" listen closely, because sometimes, that's just another way of saying, "*I stopped dreaming a while ago.*"

Why Placeholders Are the Way They Are

Renee didn't consciously decide to stop reaching.

Once upon a time, she'd been ambitious. She'd volunteered for projects that scared her, stayed late for all the right reasons, and imagined her name on an office door. But somewhere along the way, something changed. Maybe it was a promotion she didn't get, a leader who overlooked her effort, or a company restructure that replaced possibility with paperwork. Maybe it was less obvious: the times she offered an idea that no one acknowledged or when the new manager took credit for work she'd quietly perfected.

> **Each disappointment left a tiny dent. Not big enough to break her, just enough to make her more cautious. And over time, that caution started to feel like wisdom.**

Don't get your hopes up.

Stay where you're good.

Better safe than sorry.

Renee learned that competence got you more than courage. That being reliable earned gratitude, and gratitude, while not glamorous, was at least predictable. She never built confidence in herself beyond the role she already knew how to perform, so she clung to it, mistaking familiarity for her limit. She stopped pursuing "what's next" and started mastering "what's always." It was easier that way. Less chance of failure. Less chance of being seen trying, yet not quite making it.

> **And there's another truth, one harder to admit: She's built her value around being the one who knows, the one who remembers, the one who holds the threads others keep dropping.**

It feels a little like disappearing if she even thinks of letting someone else figure out those details.

People like Renee have constructed a soft, padded room built out of "I'm fine, really."

She's stuck because she failed at succeeding and slowly convinced herself that this was all she was ever meant to want.

The Link

Renee figures largely across the Enneagram, the Big Five, DiSC, and CliftonStrengths as deceptively calm. No sharp spikes, no flashing red lights. Just Predictable. Peaceful. Steadfast.

On the Enneagram, she's a blend of Type 9, The Peacemaker, and Type 5, The Observer. The Peacemaker in her seeks harmony, avoiding conflict the way some people avoid rush-hour traffic. Not because she's passive, but because she learned early on that speaking up often came with friction she didn't know how to withstand. Maybe it was a well-meaning challenge to an idea she once put forward or a probing question that landed like a verdict.

Somewhere in those moments, she decided it was safer to stay steady than to risk being wrong. She values calm because predictability feels manageable, and uncertainty feels like a test she's not sure she'll pass.

In the Big Five, Renee would score moderately high in Conscientiousness, as careful, thorough, and diligent, yet low in Openness. She likes what she knows. Familiar routines give her footing in a world that is too fast and loud.

Move her into the DiSC model, and she falls squarely in the S/C quadrant: Steadiness and Conscientiousness. She's the steady pulse of reliability others lean on, the person who won't drop the ball, who will check the policy, read the fine print, and follow through long after "thank yous" have faded into expectation. The Conscientious side denotes her love of order and rules; she believes processes exist for a reason and loves their structure. But together, S and C can create a comfort loop: a rhythm of predictability that soothes even as it stifles.

Her CliftonStrengths read like a masterclass in quiet competence: Learner, Input, Intellection, Context, Restorative, Deliberative, Consistency, and Responsibility. She takes in information relentlessly, gathering context and details others don't slow down to notice because knowing has become the way she stays indispensable. These strengths make her the backbone of every team when others lose focus.

> *Put it all together, and Renee's profile reflects reliability and depth alongside a truth she doesn't often name: Stability and stagnation can feel almost identical if you stay in one place too long.*

How to Work Alongside The Placeholder

Working with someone like Renee is both a blessing and a blind spot. She's the equalizer in crazy and the invisible adhesive gluing your entire operation together. When others are flustered, she's composed. When someone forgets a detail, no worries! She already fixed it three days ago. But here's the thing about people like Renee: they'll shoulder the load forever if you let them.

If you lead her, you might think she doesn't need much. She rarely complains, nods in meetings, delivers every task, and never seems rattled. But that silence? It's not apathy. It's restraint. Renee has ideas—good ones—she just won't volunteer them unless she's absolutely certain they'll land. If you want her to contribute beyond her comfort zone, you'll need to make it *okay* for her to be uncertain.

Ask for her feedback directly, but give her time to think before answering. A simple, "I'd love your opinion on this. Can you come back to me tomorrow with your thoughts?" can work wonders.

> **Being asked to show instant genius shuts her down; permission to reflect brings her best work to life.**

Every so often, introduce something new. Not a radical overhaul, but a small stretch: a chance to try a new tool, collaborate across teams, or lead a minor initiative. Frame it as a pilot or a supported stretch, not a test.

And when she does succeed, which she will, methodically celebrate her in a way that feels genuine. No confetti cannons or dramatic shoutouts in front of the whole team; that's not her scene. A personal thank you, a thoughtful note, or a remark that says, "I see what you do, and it matters," will mean infinitely more.

If you're a peer, pay attention to how often you lean on her. It's easy to default to Renee because she'll always say yes, which makes her indispensable, but it also makes her tired. Help her draw boundaries by setting your own. You don't have to fix her habit of saying yes; you just have to make it all right for her to say no.

And if you ever notice her holding onto work that no longer excites her, remind her gently that she's allowed to want more. Not because she's ungrateful, but because she's capable—as she's proven time and time again.

> **The goal isn't to change who she is; it's to remind her that reliability can coexist with growth.**

Know this: Beneath that unstoppable rhythm, Renee can still get excited about potential; it's just buried under years of being "the dependable one." The right kind of leadership will create just enough space and just enough air for her flame to catch again.

What If You Are The Placeholder?

If somewhere in your mind you heard a barely perceptible *Oh no, that's me*, be assured. You're not behind. You're not broken. You've simply been still for a very long time.

Somewhere along the line, you learned that being dependable was a form of love and that keeping everything running smoothly was the way to matter. You found peace in predictability, and maybe, without realizing it, you mistook that peace for purpose.

But you don't have to trade stability for growth. You can keep what's steady while still reaching for what's next. You can make a modest shift and evolve slowly. The tree outside your window still sways in the wind; it bends, and it moves through the seasons, and yet, it's still rooted. Follow its lead.

If you've been living on autopilot, saying yes because it's easier, staying because it's familiar, take one decision out of that mix. Sign up for the workshop you've bookmarked a dozen times. Ask to shadow a project you're curious about. Try something you might not be great at yet. Growth doesn't have to be dramatic; it just has to be *intentional*.

> **You've sacrificed years keeping the wheels on the wagon for everyone else. Maybe now, it's time to take a step for yourself.**

And when the guilt creeps in, because it will, remind yourself that wanting more doesn't make you ungrateful. It makes you alive.

I'm sorry to say, but the world doesn't need another perfectly reliable Placeholder. It needs *you*, the whole you, with your interest, your caution, your understated intellect, and your unrealized potential.

Your Next Step

If you recognized yourself in Renee, don't leave that realization sitting on the page.

Take the Invisible Work Archetype Assessment to see which pattern drives your workday, and join **The 7-Day Archetype Reset Challenge**, a guide designed to meet you where you are to help you take manageable, real steps toward career-evolving motion.

Start your reset at ChooseYouBook.com.

Until now, staying still may have kept you firmly anchored, but learning to move again might be what finally makes you *free*. Besides, you can't get anywhere dragging a lead weight behind you.

Chapter 15:

The Moment Before the Shift

"Shake It Out"
—Florence + The Machine

Maybe, by now, you've seen yourself in more than one story.

Maybe you saw flashes of your Overachiever in your late-nights at the office, or your Pleaser in your too-quick "Sure, I can take that on."

Maybe you felt the energy of The Always-On through the gust of wind that keeps everyone else at the tops of their games while you invisibly burn out.

Or the force of The Hurricane, pushing harder and faster to prove you'll never be contained.

Maybe you can't deny The Magnet's weary vigilance, as you forever wait for the next storm.

Or perhaps you found yourself in the still waters of The Place-holder, loyal, consistent, fading behind the rhythm of everyone else's needs.

> *Each archetype has its own melody, but as one they*
> *compose the same arrangement: a longing to be seen,*
> *heard, and valued without having to earn it first.*

No matter your archetype, we all begin these patterns for good reasons. They were the ways we learned to stay safe, to belong, to survive workplaces that rewarded output over authenticity and control over connection. But what once protected us has now become the weight we carry.

And that's what this part of the book is about, not judgment, but recognition.

Maybe, for the first time, you can see how invisibility doesn't just happen to you. It's a state you've unknowingly helped build. But that's the great fact about states—they are changeable.

And awareness? Well, that can change everything. Even what you didn't know you wanted to change.

You can't unsee what you've seen.

You can't unknow the truth that you deserve more than surviving your workday.

Now, we pause.

Not to rest, but to reset, to remember who you are, not your newly identified profile.

If you saw yourself in these pages, don't stop here.

Take the Invisible Work Archetype Assessment and start **The 7-Day Archetype Reset Challenge**, a short, powerful way to turn your awareness into movement.

It's all waiting for you at ChooseYouBook.com. Give yourself seven simple days to reject the patterns preventing your potential.

Seven days to step out from behind the role you've been playing.

Seven days to shift.

The stories you've just read, Anya's, Eli's, Sam's, Vicky's, Jonas', and Renee's, aren't just theirs. They are echoes of *yours*. And the moment you recognize that you can change your trajectory.

In Part 3, you'll learn where and how movement becomes momentum.

The real work begins here. Not the kind that drains you, but the kind that restores you. Invisibility isn't resolved by being louder or working harder. It's healed by coming home to yourself.

The **5 Pillars of Agency** that you're about to discover are not new lessons. They're old truths you've simply forgotten in the rush to prove yourself:

1. **Remember Who You Are**

2. **Find Your People**

3. **Speak Up**

4. **Start Before You're Ready**

5. **Reset Your Perspective**

These pillars are not steps in a program. They're a return, a way to reconnect with the part of you that's been here all along, waiting to be remembered.

You've met your patterns. You've seen how they influence your light. Now, it's time to rise, not as someone new, but as the person you were always meant to be.

On the following pages, you'll stop giving in to proclivities that run the machine of you and start *showing up*.

You will be able to finally and truly *choose you*.

All you have to do is turn the page to learn how.

I'll meet you there.

The 5 Pillars of Agency: Returning to Who You've Always Been

Chapter 16:

The Moment You Decide to Move

"A Million Dreams"
—The Greatest Showman Soundtrack

There comes a point in every journey where seeing the truth is no longer enough. The only logical next step is to take action.

By now, you've walked through some of the most tender territory of the book—you've considered the parts of yourself you learned to mute, shape, sacrifice, or hide.

Which brings us to Part 3: the threshold moment—the moment that occurs after awareness, even before action.

The moment when you can see your patterns clearly, but aren't yet sure what to do with that clarity. The moment that brought you here.

Your life shifts in Part 3.

My perspective and the way I approach every day didn't happen in a single moment of inspiration. It unfolded over years, slowly, quietly, sometimes painfully, until one day, during an argument with my husband, I heard myself think something so cruel, so dismissive, that it startled me: *What does he even see in me? I bring nothing.* It wasn't dramatic or shouted. I didn't even say it out loud, but it was enough, and the clearest evidence of how far I had drifted from myself. In that moment, I made an internal promise: *Never again.* I couldn't keep speaking to myself as though I were inconsequential. I couldn't keep diminishing my worth, even privately.

That realization didn't appear in isolation. It was shaped by being passed over for promotions I had earned, by choosing motherhood and watching my professional identity blur, by moving to another country and crying over the wrong loaf of bread, by being laid off from a job I was good at, by applying for 149 roles and hearing nothing back. Each experience pulled another thread loose until eventually, I didn't recognize the unraveled person in front of me.

> **As I spoke to friends, colleagues, and strangers who became confidants, I had an epiphany that changed everything: This feeling wasn't unique to me. It wasn't even rare.**

So many people, especially the ones who care deeply and give generously, live with a muffled sense of invisibility. They question their worth, their impact, and their place in the world. They try to manage every detail of families, teams, and organizations while slowly disappearing.

Growing invisible is happening against the backdrop of a world that feels heavier every year. Economic instability, layoffs, burnout, loneliness, rising expectations, and global uncertainty, to name a few.

But turmoil isn't the point.

This is: While the world may not steady anytime soon, you can find your footing.

In Part 3, you're not about to work on becoming a different person. You're about to come home to the person you were *before* life taught you to disappear. Before you learned to translate worth into performance. Before you took on roles that made everyone else comfortable as you underfed your identity. Before the world demanded so much and made you forget that you were allowed to ask for what you needed and wanted of it in return.

Introducing the 5 Pillars of Agency

The **5 Pillars of Agency** that follow are not quick fixes, glossy affirmations, or one-size-fits-all behaviors. They are the steady foundations that help you rebuild yourself from the inside out.

> *I have arranged these pillars in a specific order because real transformation has a sequence that begins at the core and builds outward.*

You *cannot* speak up if you don't remember who you are.

You *cannot* shift your perspective if you're surrounded by people who reinforce your doubt.

You *cannot* take brave action if you've forgotten what matters to you.

Each pillar prepares you for what's next and closes a gap created somewhere in the earlier parts of your story. In the chapters ahead, we will explore:

Pillar 1: Remember Who You Are – The foundation. Here, you'll peel back the layers shaped by family, culture, work, and survival. You'll reconnect with the values, strengths, and truths that have always been there, just waiting to be reclaimed.

Pillar 2: Find Your People – The circle. Confidence doesn't grow in isolation. We all need people who hold up a mirror and say, "I see you," especially when we forget how to see ourselves.

Pillar 3: Speak Up – The bridge. I am not encouraging you to speak up to be louder or dominate, but to use your voice with clarity and intention, planted in identity rather than insecurity.

Pillar 4: Start Before You're Ready – The action. Waiting for confidence is one of the most common ways we disappear. Momentum builds self-belief—not the other way around.

Pillar 5: Reset Your Perspective – The renewal. Here, you'll learn to reinterpret setbacks, widen your view, and create room for empathy, grace, and growth. You'll stop reacting to your life and start participating in it again.

In the coming chapters, you'll read about research woven into stories, practical steps blended with reflection, and psychological observations drawn from years of studying human behavior and decades of watching how it actually shows up at work and in life. This isn't a textbook; it's a toolkit, one honoring the science of human behavior and the humanity of real people navigating real lives.

> *If Part 1 helped you understand how you got lost, and Part 2 showed you how that loss shows up at work, then Part 3 is where you start the road back to return to yourself.*

You've already done the courageous work of naming the patterns and recognizing the masks to see where the light has faltered within you. Now, it's time to rebuild. To step back into your life with intention, clarity, and a steadying sense of self you can trust.

It's time to stop disappearing and begin again.

One pillar at a time.

Chapter 17:

Pillar 1—Remember Who You Are

"This Is Me"
—The Greatest Showman Soundtrack

The moment forgetting hits you usually begins with a question so harmless you barely notice it at first.

Someone, maybe a colleague, is making polite small talk in your midst, maybe it's a new acquaintance with great posture and suspiciously tidy hair, who asks, "So ... what do you do for fun?"

For a split second, everything inside you stills.

Your mind, normally a bustling marketplace of to-do lists, half-remembered conversations, and the lingering shame of something you said in 2008, suddenly offers ... nothing but ...

A blank screen.

A buffering wheel.

An empty stage with a spotlight.

"Oh, you know," you begin almost automatically. "I love spending time with my family. And catching up with friends, we always have the best laughs ..."

You smile. You nod. You deliver the lines effortlessly, like someone reading from a script they've performed so many times they barely need the cue cards.

Even as the words wind their way out of your mouth, you can't help thinking, *That's not really it, is it?*

Then, you can't stop an even more intrusive thought: *Come on. That can't be your entire answer.*

Can you relate?

When did your preferences become a collage of other people's passions?

When did your free time turn into something you curated for the sake of sounding balanced, agreeable, and well-rounded?

When did what makes you feel alive quietly get replaced by what you feel responsible for?

You might hear yourself wonder, *When did I begin blurting out the "right" answer instead of telling people what I really think?*

Now, you're stuck with the unsettling awareness that you've been inching away from yourself for a long time without meaning to.

> **And there, in that tiny pause between your practiced answer and your inner truth, something dawns on you:**

You don't remember what you like anymore.

That is the moment you realize, it's time to come home to yourself.

What Pillar 1 Really Means

Remembering who you are isn't the kind of transformation people like to romanticize. It's not a plane ticket to a remote mountain lodge where you spend a week in silence, hiking through pine-scented air, journaling beside a waterfall, and eating food that tastes suspiciously like discipline disguised as vegetables. It isn't a spiritual vision, a sudden download from the universe, or the kind of thunderclap movies would have you believe arrives at the perfect cinematic moment.

It's the slow realization that somewhere between all the roles you've played: parent, partner, professional, and friend, you've stopped hearing your own voice clearly. Not because it disappeared, but because it was drowned out by everything you needed to be for everyone else. You became fluent in supporting, in adjusting, in carrying more than your share ... and as that fluency grew, your connection to yourself thinned until you hardly noticed it disappearing.

> *Pillar 1 peels away the expectations and obligations long enough to ask: What matters to me? What feels true? What feels like home?*

These questions aren't just philosophical.

There is an emotional cost to losing contact with yourself that often shows up long before you can recognize it. When you've lived too long on autopilot or performing the version of yourself the world seems to expect, your mind protects you in unsettling ways.

Subtle detachment creeps in. There you are, just living your life, technically present, amidst a layer of fog muddying up the distance between you and the present moment.

Psychologists describe the extreme end of this experience as depersonalization or derealization: It's the disjointed sense that you're watching your life rather than living it. Most people never reach this clinical threshold, yet many experience similar stages: moving through a day robotically, struggling to feel joy, sensing numbness where enthusiasm used to be, or losing track of their opinions because they've become so accustomed to molding themselves around what's needed. These aren't failures of character. They are signals—your mind's quiet way of saying, *I need you to come back to me.*

> **That is why this pillar comes first. Before you can choose the right people, speak with any kind of conviction, take brave action, or flip your perspective, you need a stable center to come home to.**

You need to know you. A life built on a blurry sense of self becomes a life of exhausting decisions, where boundaries feel impossible, and your voice sounds uncertain even to you. But a life built on a remembered self becomes a self you can articulate, trust, and inhabit. It feels steadier, more grounded, more yours.

This work is not about reinventing yourself. It's meeting the you who followed instinct again. The you who felt connected to your own desires, whether they made sense to anyone else or not.

Remembering who you are is your invitation to explore again, slowly and with curiosity rather than judgment. It is the rediscovery of a relationship that was never truly broken, only neglected. The moment you turn back toward yourself, even slightly, life sharpens.

You stop floating above your days and start dropping back into them, capable of making decisions and tapping into your gut. You feel present again, not in a grand, transformative way, but in the certainty that you are here, in this life, as yourself.

Everything else you want to accomplish, and your reclaimed identity builds from here and depends on your connections, your voice, and your courage.

The Practice

Before you go any further, grab something you can write with. A pen, a notebook, the back of a receipt, your Notes app, anything.

This part of the journey isn't meant to stay in your head. It needs to be written down, so your thoughts become tangible and real.

And if you haven't already done so, check out ChooseYouBook.com and take the How Invisible Are You at Work? Quiz. Not because quizzes are magical, but because your personalized report will become the companion that travels with you. Your report will include the exercises, reflections, tools, and links that can deepen everything we're about to explore. This book will guide you, but the report will anchor you.

You might find, at first, that writing feels awkward, even indulgent. You might stare at the blank page and think, *What am I supposed to say? What if I say it wrong?* As if there is a way to be incorrect about yourself. But that hesitation is part of the remembering. It's a sign that your inner world hasn't been asked to speak freely in a long time.

Start slowly.

Think of a moment in your life where you felt unmistakably alive. I'm talking about one of those unexpected flashes where your body was open, your mind was clear, and for a few seconds, you weren't performing or pleasing or proving. You were simply *you*. My moment is every moment I ever lost myself on a dance floor. Late nights, music too loud, dancing until the sun came up.

Now, it's your turn.

What is your moment?

What did the air smell like?

What were your hands doing?

What was the expression on your face?

Did time feel slow or fast?

Your senses will remember long before your logic does.

If nothing comes, that's not failure. That's information and an invitation to slow down a little more.

You can try what helped me.

One morning, before the rest of the house woke up, I sat cross-legged on the carpet with my palms open on my knees. I closed my eyes and pictured three memories that made gratitude flood my whole body, the kind that warms your chest from the inside out. And as they tripped across my mind, my shoulders relaxed, a smile spread across my face, and I could almost hear a younger version of myself confirm: *There you are.*

My memories didn't fix anything, but they pointed me toward the parts of myself I had neglected. I remembered the projects that had gone exceptionally well. They had earned real praise. They mattered. (*And they were a success.*) But somewhere along the way, I stopped remembering why. I knew the outcome. I knew the win, but I'd forgotten my role in it. I couldn't remember what it was about how I'd led, how I'd thought, how I'd approached the work that made those projects great. I hadn't forgotten the success. I'd forgotten myself inside it.

Once your memories start to surface, you'll find it easier to write. You might feel pulled to jot down words, phrases, moments, and familiar pieces of yourself.

Let them come without editing. This is not a performance; this is a reunion.

As you continue, you may want to gather additional tools to help you see yourself clearly again.

Personality assessments, for instance, aren't meant to tell you who you are. They are conversation starters. I once spent weeks reading through my results with a highlighter, noticing which phrases made me smile unexpectedly, which strengths I'd forgotten I had, and which tendencies felt like relief to acknowledge. I wrote in the margins. I circled the parts of myself I had minimized for years because they didn't fit compactly into the version of me the world seemed to prefer.

Two small lists I wrote out changed everything.

One was titled: "*I am good at.*"

And another: "I *believe in* ..." I jotted down five items in each list. They were not polished, not impressive, and not edited for public consumption. They were just true and just for me.

As I wrote them, facets of myself returned. I keep those lists on my whiteboard now, and on days when I feel unsteady, I glance at them and think, *Yes. That's me. I remember.*

You might write your lists in a notebook, pin them above your desk, or type them into your phone so they're always close. There is no correct way to do this. There is only the way that brings you back to yourself.

And then, there is the practice that most people avoid: sitting with your own thoughts long enough to hear beneath the noise. Journaling without filters. Asking questions like:

1. *When did I feel most like myself today?*

2. *Where did I disappear?*

3. *What did my body try to tell me?*

4. *What truth was I afraid to admit, even to myself?*

5. *What am I proud of, even if no one else noticed?*

You might believe, at first, that you won't have any answers, that the questions will float in the air unanswered, or worse, that they'll expose a blankness you're afraid to confront, but answers always come.

> **Your mind has been waiting years for you to turn toward it with genuine curiosity instead of criticism, and it will offer you pieces of yourself as soon as it senses you're ready to hold them.**

Pillar 1 is not about getting the practice right or producing pages of profound insight. It's about building the muscle of remembering, returning to yourself again and again until your inner world no longer feels like a stranger you occasionally bump into, but a place you recognize and move through with ease. With each sentence you write, with each memory, with each realization that rises to the surface, you are relighting a small torch inside yourself. Individually, these torches are subtle. Together, they illuminate the path you've been craving, the path that leads you back to a steadier, truer sense of who you are.

As you return to the notebook, as you return to the memory of you, this is where the real work begins. As you return to the parts of yourself you muzzled because you stopped asking about them, keep working at it, and you will feel the foundation beneath you again, not the borrowed one you've been standing on for years, but the solid one that belongs only to you.

So, yes, keep writing. Keep listening. Keep returning. In these small, steady acts, you are rebuilding the foundation of you.

The Barriers and Breakthroughs

It's tempting to believe that once you decide to reconnect with yourself, the process will unfold naturally, as if clarity will arrive simply because you've invited it. But anyone who has ever tried to slow down long enough to hear their own voice knows it isn't that simple. Certain barriers are built into the way we live, and they have a way of yanking you back toward old patterns.

One of the first challenges you will face in this process is sitting with a blank page. It can show up as a sudden urge to check your phone, to straighten the counter, to answer an email that absolutely could have waited. Beneath those distractions is a deeper discomfort: the fear that if you look inward, you may discover what you've been avoiding; You may have to admit that you're tired in a way that sleep can't solve or lonely in a way that company can't reach or dissatisfied in places where you've convinced yourself to settle. It can feel easier to stay busy than to face the possibility that something in your life may need to be altered.

There is also a simmering script many of us grew up with that teaches us that self-reflection is indulgent.

> *Many of us were raised with the message that tending to your own needs is selfish, that you should be grateful for what you have, that asking "What do I want?" is a luxury reserved for people with too much time on their hands.*

When you've internalized those beliefs, turning inward to finally serve yourself can feel wrong, as though claiming space in your own life is an act of rebellion rather than a necessary return.

> *And perhaps the most significant barrier is that forgetting yourself often happens so gradually that reclaiming yourself feels unfamiliar.*

On the other side of that initial discomfort lies a breakthrough that rarely comes from anything external. It might be a moment of unexpected ease in a conversation or a once-agonizing decision feeling clear. You'll note that your choices are aligning with your true desires rather than the person you felt obligated to be. Then, you'll sense the pride that grows from making decisions rooted in authenticity, even when those decisions seem pretty minor.

Over time, the benefits can compound. Your relationships can deepen because people will finally be interacting with the real you, not your adapted version. Your confidence will also strengthen because it now has a foundation built on *your* values, *your* strengths, and *your* preferences. Even your ambitions become clearer; it is difficult to pursue what you truly want when you don't know who you are, but once you reconnect with yourself, your desires sharpen into focus.

Most surprising of all, perhaps, is the sense of relief that comes from no longer performing your way through your life. When you remember who you are, you stop waiting for others to validate your choices. You stop living outside yourself. A groundedness grows from this work; it's not flashy and not dramatic, but it is unmistakably yours. You can return to your life as an active participant, not a quiet observer.

That is the breakthrough worth fighting for. It's not a new personality or a reinvention that impresses the world, but a steady, honest alignment that makes everything else, every boundary, every brave conversation, every step forward, feel possible again.

Your Next Step

At this point in the chapter, remembering has already begun. The next step is simply to continue that motion deliberately and without rushing.

Start simple: Choose a personality assessment from Truity.com. Take it with curiosity and the intention of noticing what you can relate to. When you read your results, highlight the phrases that make you smile unexpectedly, the ones articulating a truth you forgot. Make notes in the margins. Circle the strengths you downplay. Let the description be a doorway, not a definition, an opening into parts of yourself you haven't visited in a while.

Then, when you're ready, put pen to paper again—this time, to list out these magnificent parts of yourself.

You don't need to write pages of reflection if that feels overwhelming. You can begin with the same two lists that helped me reconnect with myself when everything felt scattered.

At the top of the first page, write: "*I am good at,*" and permit yourself to fill it out slowly. Think of what comes naturally to you, what people come to you for, what makes you proud. You might write down obvious characteristics or those that are small and easily overlooked. Both count.

On the next page, write: "*I believe in ...*" These are your values, the lines you won't cross, the truths about yourself that stay locked in place even when everything else doesn't. They don't need to impress anyone. They just need to be yours.

If you need help getting started, try asking yourself:

1. *When do I feel most like myself?*

2. *What qualities do I admire in myself, even if I rarely say them out loud?*

3. *What moments make me feel grounded, present, or alive?*

If writing is challenging, but you respond to a guided meditation, for instance, try that.

MotivationHub's *LISTEN EVERY DAY! Guided Meditation for Success, Wealth and Happiness* is simple, accessible, grounding, and free on YouTube. If you're ready to go deeper, explore the teachings of Eckhart Tolle or Moojiji, who can help you hear what you've lost touch with inside yourself.

Whatever path you choose: reflection, writing, meditation, or all three, permit yourself to move at your own pace. Remember, rediscovering who you are is not a race. Again, it's a return.

And finally, before you close this chapter, take the How Invisible Are You at Work? Quiz at ChooseYouBook.com. Your personalized report will walk you through exercises, prompts, reflections, and resources that deepen everything we've explored here. Think of it as a way to keep this work alive long after you turn the page.

This is the beginning of your return to yourself, the rebuilding of your inner foundation.

All caused by small, intentional steps.

After reading this far, you're already on your way.

Chapter 18:

Pillar 2—Find Your People

"From Now On"
—The Greatest Showman Soundtrack

The Moment You Realize You're in the Wrong Room

The truth can sneak up in the most ordinary of places.

You're standing in someone's kitchen, balancing a paper plate of snacks in one hand and a lukewarm drink in the other. Small talk froths around you: kids' schedules, weekend plans, a new series on Netflix that apparently everyone has seen except you. People laugh in little bursts. Someone brushes past you to get to the guacamole.

From the outside, you look like you're part of it. You nod in the right places. You add a comment here and there. You laugh when everyone else does.

But inside, you can't escape a troubling question:

If I disappeared from this room right now, would anyone actually notice?

Not "notice" in the polite, "Oh, where did she go?" way. "Notice," so that people felt a loss, a void where you were standing.

You glance around and realize you can name these people's children, their job titles, the suburb they live in ... but you're not sure any of them know what keeps *you* up at night. You're not sure who, in this whole space, you would text if a truly big event happened. The good big. The terrible big. The "I just need someone to sit in this with me" big.

This can't be it. This can't be what having "people" feels like.

At the beginning of this book, I shared that it took me until I was 12 to feel like I had an actual friend. Not a classmate. Not a convenient bus-stop companion. A friend. Someone who *chose me.* I wish I could tell you that once I had that friend who wanted me around, the whole "finding your people" thing was simple from then on.

It wasn't.

Which leads me to Pillar 2. And if I'm being totally honest with you, it just might be the hardest pillar.

I know what it feels like to think you've found your forever person in friendship, only to lose her later, and not to death. Just because, as happens, you've drifted. You've unfriended each other or been unfriended, and not on social media, but in real life. So, I still see her posts. I still know when her kids have birthdays. But the version of me that used to send the first voice note, that used to be on the other end of that call, no longer exists in her world. The grief of that is real, even if nobody around you names it.

I know what it feels like to be in the wrong circles, too.

The ones where "How's your *little* business going?" sounds casual on the surface but lands like a stone in your stomach. Where the group laughs about "corporate dreams," and you join in, because what else do you do? Even though all the while inside you're thinking, *I actually care about this. This matters to me. Why am I minimizing it to make everyone else more comfortable?*

The better news?

I also know what it feels like to rebuild your self-belief brick by brick after comments like that. To tell yourself, They don't get it, and to finally believe that you do.

I also know how different it feels when you are truly supported.

I know the warmth when someone messages you on launch day, not to say, "Good luck," but "I booked time in my calendar to watch you because this is big." When a friend hears your idea and instead of asking, "Are you sure?" simply says, "Of course, you can do this." When you get a brutal email or gut-punch feedback and can rely on one or two people that you send a screenshot to with the caption: "Tell me I'm not insane," and then they respond with the perfect mix of honesty and protection.

Right now, as I write this, there are two people in my life who are not family, not my husband, not anyone who is obligated to be here, who show up like that for me. Two. Not 20. Not a sprawling, glossy Instagram grid of besties on girls' trips. A tiny, fiercely loyal handful.

Adult friendship often doesn't look like the dream we were sold.

A cultural picture of what "finding your people" is supposed to be: long wooden tables under fairy lights, group vacations in matching linen, and monthly book clubs where everyone actually reads the book permeates society. Sure, sometimes that happens. But often, real friendship looks like a five-minute voice note between meetings. A random meme at 11:43 p.m. A "thinking of you" text when you haven't seen each other in months.

It's phone calls taken in messy kitchens, not curated coffee dates. It's showing up when life is falling apart, not just when there's a fun get-together on the calendar.

And yet, even if you're fortunate enough to have all that, there's still that moment.

The one where you catch yourself scrolling through your phone, realizing you're not sure who to message. The one where you notice that your most active group chat is with colleagues, not friends. The one where you realize that if something wonderful happened, you'd announce it on LinkedIn before you'd tell an actual person you trust.

Pillar 2 is dedicated to the moment when you can finally admit to yourself, *I'm lonely. Not for more people. For my people.*

> **If remembering who you are is about coming home to yourself, then finding your people is about making sure you don't have to live there alone.**

What Pillar 2 Really Means

Finding your people isn't about increasing the number of humans in your orbit. It's about recognizing that belonging is a basic psychological need, stitched into us long before we learned to speak.

Modern research keeps reaffirming what we feel instinctively: Loneliness is not just uncomfortable, it's dangerous.

The U.S. Surgeon General identifies chronic disconnection as a public health concern, noting that sustained loneliness activates the same regions of the brain that register physical pain. Isolation doesn't just weigh on your heart; it burdens your nervous system, your memory, your immunity, and your sense of self.

Belonging isn't created by simply having company. That's the part most of us misunderstand.

We live in a time when digital connection is abundant and true connection is scarce. We can be constantly in touch and never feel truly bonded with anyone. You can have a full calendar, dozens of contacts, hundreds of interactions, and still feel alone in a room.

Your people, the real ones, fall outside that definition or analogy.

They are the ones whose presence strengthens your sense of who you are rather than diluting it. The ones who don't flinch when you speak honestly. The ones who don't feel threatened in the presence of your ambition or collapse under the weight of your vulnerability.

Trevor Noah has talked about how the people who shaped him most weren't the ones with all the answers, but the ones who created space for him to be more himself. Oprah describes true friendship as the place where you can finally breathe out, where the performance ends and the truth begins.

This is why the first pillar had to come before this one. Once you start remembering who you are, you begin to notice, sometimes painfully, who helps you stay connected to that self and who pulls you away from it. Some relationships were built around the version of you that stayed agreeable and convenient. As you grow, those dynamics feel like clothes you've steadily outgrown.

Adult friendships are notoriously difficult, not because we are incapable of connection, but because our modern lives are structured in ways that make vulnerability inconvenient. Remote work keeps us physically apart. Social media keeps us performing. Busyness keeps us distracted. Pride keeps us distant. Loneliness proliferates under all of it.

> **When we talk about finding our people, I mean choosing connections that are intentional, not accidental. And not just convenient. Not based solely on proximity or shared history.**

It's recognizing that the people in your life shape your courage, your clarity, your ambition, and your resilience. They influence the risks you take and the dreams you allow yourself to pursue.

Neuroscience studies prove that the brain literally changes in the presence of safe relationships. Meaningful connection stabilizes your emotional systems and strengthens your ability to navigate stress, uncertainty, and growth. You think differently, decide differently, and recover differently when you're not bracing your way through life alone.

Pillar 2 allows you to build relationships that make you braver, steadier, clearer, and more fully yourself—relationships where you don't have to ration your joy or translate your dreams into a more digestible version. Relationships that don't drain you or diminish you, but expand you.

Not *more* people.

Your people.

The ones who make the journey back to yourself feel not just possible, but supported.

The Practice

Finding your people begins long before you ever speak to anyone. It starts with noticing, really noticing, what happens inside your body as you move through the world. Before you change anything in your outer circle, tune into your inner signals.

The U.S. Surgeon General's Advisory on social connection reminds us that it's the quality of our relationships and how seen and supported we feel that matters most. Those reactions are data, not drama. They point you toward where connection might naturally grow.

Once you begin paying attention in this way, you'll find yourself drawn to making minor, intentional gestures toward the people filling you up. Nothing grand. Nothing performative. Just suggestive openings that signal: "I am here, and I'm willing to be seen." You might send a thoughtful message to someone whose insight genuinely moved you. Maybe you'll add a personal note when replying to a colleague or share more honesty than defaulting to your usual: "All good, thanks."

Dr. Julianne Holt-Lunstad's research on social connection shows that even brief, supportive interactions can activate our neural pathways associated with trust and belonging. In other words, tiny moments matter more than we think.

Then there's the power of consistent contact. Dr. Jeffrey Hall's work on friendship hours reveals that genuine friendship rarely appears out of nowhere; it emerges through repeated touchpoints rather than occasional grand gestures. Part of this practice is showing up, not in a forced "networking" way, but with an open attitude to forge any connection with the potential to repeat itself naturally.

Let's say you join a shared-interest group and attend its gatherings more than once. You then return to the same online community thread instead of lurking and leaving. The spaces where you appear consistently become the spaces where others recognize you, and recognition is the first root tendril of belonging.

> *As you move in this way, you change. You listen differently. You notice when someone reveals a telling truth and respond with care instead of quickly moving on.*

You let conversations expand beyond shallow. You allow humor, curiosity, and humanity to enter places where you once stayed overly polished.

Sometimes all it takes is one earnest sentence to create an opening.

You can also start choosing your circles more deliberately. Not every group will be for you, and that's okay. Maybe you want to be part of a professional community where ambition is normalized rather than mocked. Maybe you're longing for a creative space where vulnerability is welcomed. Maybe your new group is defined by a life stage, identity, or a cause that authentically matters to you.

Research on social connection shows that shared meaning accelerates intimacy. We attach faster to people who care about what we care about, not because they reflect us, but because we feel understood at a deeper level.

Slowly, as you practice these burgeoning acts of reaching outward, you may begin to sense the difference between people who feel familiar and people who feel *true*. Familiarity is about proximity; truth is about resonance. The practice of finding your people is learning to trust that resonance, recognizing when a conversation leaves you feeling more like yourself, and figuring out how to follow the filaments of connection that lead you unmistakably toward something far more meaningful.

Keep at it until one day, when you realize you've undergone a subtle transformation. Your world may not look fuller from the outside, but it can feel more solid on the inside. You have begun gathering the beginnings of real connection. Not the glossy version of adult friendship we see online, but the grounded, nourishing, ordinary kind that supports your everyday life more.

You're not chasing or performing. You're simply paying attention, offering invitations, and allowing the right people to find their way toward you as you find your way toward them.

The Barriers and Breakthroughs

For all the beauty that comes with meaningful connection, Pillar 2 is often the one people stumble over the most. Not because they don't want deeper friendships, but because the path to those friendships asks for what we're out of practice giving: vulnerability, initiative, consistency, and courage.

Most adults are bruised in this area, caused by friendships that withered without explanation, betrayals they didn't see coming, and/or circles where they never quite fit. Those memories don't disappear; they shape how quickly we reach for others and how much of ourselves we're willing to offer.

One of the most common barriers to overcome is the simple fear of going first.

Social psychologist Vanessa Bohns calls this the "liking gap." It's the well-documented finding that people consistently underestimate how much others enjoy their company. In her research, participants assumed that initiating a conversation or reaching out would make them seem intrusive or needy, when in reality, others perceived them as warm, likable, and welcome. The fear is internal; the barrier is imagined, but the impact of connection is real; however, we continue to stay silent even when connection is entirely possible.

Layered on top of that assumption is the belief that everyone else already has their circle. Simon Sinek has described the quiet loneliness of adulthood as a kind of collective waiting game: Everyone wants close friendships, but no one wants to be the one *who appears to need them*. So, we sit in our separate corners, telling ourselves we're the only ones feeling disconnected, when in truth, most adults feel the same, even those whose external lives look full.

And don't forget the power of the residue of past hurt. Losing a friendship you believed would last forever creates a very specific kind of grief that most people carry. It makes you cautious, even if you won't admit it out loud.

Brené Brown's research on vulnerability shows that emotional risk is harder for people who have been burned before because their minds equate openness with danger. As a result, we distance ourselves just enough to avoid the possibility of loss, not realizing that this distance prevents the possibility of closeness.

If reading these past few pages has got you down, don't lose heart, because on the other side of these barriers is a breakthrough impossible to replicate through self-work alone.

Your support doesn't need to come from many, either. Robin Dunbar's work reminds us that humans are wired for a very small inner circle—we need just three to five people with whom emotional closeness is strongest.

> **So, *when you find one or two who genuinely celebrate you, who don't feel the need to trample your ambition or diminish your joy, who don't flinch when you need honesty cushioned in love, the effect is enormous.***

For many people, that tiny circle becomes a stabilizing force, a place to land, a place to be seen, a place to be reminded of who they are when life tries to convince them otherwise.

And the most surprising breakthrough?

Connection creates momentum. Once you experience the safety of a relationship where you can breathe easily, you show up differently everywhere else. You take more risks. You speak more honestly. You hold your boundaries more cleanly. You pursue the opportunities you once talked yourself out of. Confidence doesn't grow in isolation; it prospers in reflection, in the steady presence of people who remind you that you are capable, even on the days you forget.

Pillar 2 isn't just about friendship. It's about the psychological, emotional, and even physical transformation that becomes possible when you stop trying to carry your entire life alone. Because when you find even a few of your people, you move through the world with more support and the courage that comes only from being held and accepted exactly as you are.

Your Next Step

By now, you probably feel a new sensation waking up inside you. It's not dramatic, but it is an unmistakable awareness, telling you that maybe you don't need more people; you just need the right ones. It is the understanding that connection won't fall into your lap the way it sometimes did when you were younger. That now, as an adult, you must play a more active role in shaping the circle that shapes you.

Here's where you begin.

Take little steps, so your nervous system won't mistake movement as threat. Think of someone whose presence lingers with you long after a conversation ends, someone who makes you feel lighter, seen, or unexpectedly energized. There is always at least one person you might be discounting. Maybe it was a colleague who asked the kind of question that made you feel interesting. Maybe it was someone you met at a workshop or in a webinar. Maybe it was the person whose post you saved because their tone rang a bell you hadn't heard in a long time.

Reach out to them.

Not with a dramatic confession about needing a deeper friendship, but with a written smile: "This made me think of you." "I loved what you shared in that meeting." "Let me know if you ever want to chat again." These tiny gestures are the building blocks of connection.

As you do this, you widen your world just a little.

In my own life, moving countries forced me into the humility of starting from scratch. I didn't know anyone, so I joined groups, not because they were perfect matches, but because they gave me even a little snippet of what I was missing. The mom group wasn't my space, but the entrepreneurial one was. Sometimes, you find your people by first touching base with the wrong ones and learning to adjust. Consistency, not perfection, creates a soil that cultivates friendship.

And then there's the part of my journey that still surprises me when I say it out loud: One year, I started messaging strangers on LinkedIn—people I admired but had absolutely no business "DM-ing" according to every rule of adult etiquette. I introduced myself, told them I was new in the U.S., and asked if they'd be open to sharing what they'd learned about working here. I didn't script a perfect message. I didn't pretend to be more established than I was.

I just. Reached. Out.

Some never responded.

But some did.

And those "some" altered the trajectory of my life.

A few of them are now partners in my business. A handful are friends who check in on the days I feel shaky. All of them are proof that courage creates connection long before confidence does.

Perhaps your next step is to make one small ask.

One coffee.

One conversation.

One message sent even though your finger hovered an extra five seconds before sending it out into space.

And while you experiment with these openings, pay close attention to what your body tells you afterward. Real connection doesn't leave you feeling like you want to run away or that you have to hide under the rug. It doesn't leave you doubting your worth or rehashing every sentence you ever spoke. It leaves you more yourself.

As you navigate these early steps, it may help to reflect on your existing circles. Ask yourself:

Who drains you?

Who dismisses you?

Who makes you hold back your dreams or rework your truth?

You don't have to sever ties dramatically; you can simply loosen your grip, inch by inch, and redirect your energy toward the places where you are allowed to grow.

> **And if you feel overwhelmed because this part of the work tends to reopen old wounds, let your next step be to recognize that you're not alone in this. Adult connection is difficult for nearly everyone. You're not behind or unfixable. You're human.**

To support you as you take these steps, I've created a resource that goes deeper than I can cover in a single chapter. The How Invisible Are You at Work? Quiz at ChooseYouBook.com will give you a personalized report that includes guided reflection prompts, micro-actions for building meaningful connection, and practical ways to expand or refine your circle. It's not a shortcut, but a compass to keep yourself aligned as you move ahead.

Remember:

You are not searching for an audience.

You are searching for allies.

For the people who hold equal space for your truth and your ambition.

The end of this chapter marks the beginning of finding your new group.

And, in time, the beginning of you being found.

Chapter 19:

Pillar 3—Speak Up

"The Greatest Show"
—The Greatest Showman Soundtrack

The Moment Silence Stops Working

I had just stepped into my new Learning & Development manager role, which came with a big team, big remuneration, and big expectations. A month later, I found myself sitting across from my manager asking, "What will it take for me to get my next promotion?"

He laughed good-naturedly in that "Oh, *you're already thinking ahead*" way managers sometimes do. "Candice, you've been in the role for five minutes, and you're already asking about the next one?"

But I wasn't asking for it now. I just didn't want to wake up two years later and realize I'd been running hard in the wrong direction and working diligently on the wrong goals. So, I held my ground.

"I'm asking because I want to be ready when the time comes. If the next move is two years away, I need to start now."

We constructed a reasonable plan on paper: Be a top performer, develop myself, stay visible, and deliver real impact. Simple. Achievable. A little too neat. But I didn't question it then. I took that list as gospel, tucked it under my arm like homework no one else had been brave enough to ask for, and for the next two years, I checked off every single item on it.

I accomplished it all. Not halfway. Not modestly.

I became the "walk on water" performer, the rating people joked didn't exist. That Performance Rating had to be signed off by the CEO because it was so unusual for someone that new in a role. I was selected for a global leadership program, one of only nine people out of twelve thousand across the organization. My inbox buzzed with people saying, "This is huge," "You're really going places," and "You've made it."

I was moved from one function to another to "lift up" a struggling department because my current one was so strong. On every metric, on every chart, on every performance calibration slide, it looked like the universe was quietly placing stepping stones in front of me. All I had to do was keep walking.

So, when the Learning & Development director role for the sales division opened, and it was the dream job tailored to everything I cared about, I didn't hesitate. I prepared with the kind of obsessive energy reserved for aims that feel both within reach *and* life-changing. My presentation was tight. My examples were strong. My results were undeniable. Even now, I look back at those slides and think, *That was a damn good interview deck.*

I walked into that room confident, steady, ready.

And then, after my interview ended, I stepped into the hallway and saw Ashley standing there.

She cradled a box of learning materials in her arms, a tangible, look-what-I've-done prop we all instinctively know matters in corporate rooms. As she held it with ease, her poise suggested that she hadn't agonized over whether she deserved to be here. One look at her face, and you knew that she believed she belonged.

Inside that box was work I had created: programs, templates, frameworks, and content all built from scratch. She did iterate on it, yes. She did add her own flavor, but those were my bones. When she left me in the hallway to walk into the room carrying physical proof of the work I had done, my whole body reacted.

Not dramatically. Not theatrically. I readied for impact, like a stone hitting water far deeper than you expected.

They're going to give it to her, a voice in my head nickered. *They're going to give her the job.*

I stifled my tears long enough to reach my car. The second the door closed, my façade crumbled, and I cried the whole way home, my chest wrenching, recognizing the truth before my brain could say it out loud.

It wasn't losing the job that broke me. It was the process of under-standing *why*.

I had followed the rules.

I had done everything asked of me.

I had waited patiently, humbly, and politely for my work to speak for itself.

Meanwhile, Ashley *had* spoken. She *had* advocated for herself. She *had* made her work visible. She *had* built relationships I hadn't prioritized because I *had* thought "doing great work" was the only relationship I needed. In that moment, watching her stride into the room with my work in her hands, I finally understood the lesson I should have learned years earlier:

Doing excellent work isn't enough if no one knows you're the one doing it.

That night, sitting across from my then-boyfriend (now-husband) at my favorite restaurant, he tried to reassure me. "You're overreacting. There's no way they'll choose her. You're 10 times better. They'll see that."

But I knew they wouldn't. And I was right.

When the decision came, it confirmed what I had already processed in that hallway: *I wasn't seen as the obvious choice because I hadn't made myself visible as the obvious choice.*

> **I had left my career in the hands of good intentions, organizational memory, and the hope that someone somewhere was keeping track of the effort I had poured in.**

No one was.

Because that was never their job.

It was mine.

That was the moment Pillar 3 really began to take shape; it was not born in anger or bitterness, but in a sharp, clarifying realization:

I keep waiting to be chosen in a system that only moves in my direction when I choose myself.

Advocating for yourself isn't arrogance. It's alignment. It's truth-telling. It's refusing to outsource your career to people busy managing their own. It's the movement from hoping to be noticed to taking responsibility for making your work, your voice, and your value undeniable.

Once you put that into play, you can't go back.

What Pillar 3 Really Means

Speaking up is one of those concepts that sounds so simple in theory that we underestimate the seismic shift it requires in practice. For most of us, it doesn't begin as a bold declaration, but as an understated understanding that the strategies we were raised on: work hard, be humble, keep your head down, let the results speak for themselves, are not actually strategies. They are a woven comfort blanket, one that frays the moment you realize how decisions are really made inside organizations.

Self-advocacy is not about self-promotion, arrogance, or taking up space for the sake of taking up space.

It is the deeply human act of refusing to outsource your career to luck, timing, or someone else's memory of your contributions. It is the moment you stop living under the illusion that being good is the same as being visible. Research tells us that visibility matters as much as competence. Sometimes more.

For decades, organizational psychologists have studied how leaders do not make decisions solely based on performance. They make decisions based on *perceived* performance, recognized impact, and relational trust. What they can't see, they can't reward. What they don't know you want, they can't offer. What you downplay, they assume must not matter. It isn't malicious; it's human nature. Cognitive load means leaders default to what's right in front of them.

That's why quietly hoping someone will "notice" you often leads to the exact opposite.

In addition, there is surprisingly little research on self-advocacy compared to other professional development topics. You can find thousands of articles on leadership, emotional intelligence, communication, and teamwork ... but when it comes to speaking up for your worth, your ideas, or your career? The literature becomes remarkably thin. Maybe that's because most workplaces don't want to encourage self-advocacy. It disrupts hierarchy. It requires transparency. It demands clarity around development and opportunity. It forces leaders to articulate decisions they often prefer to keep ambiguous.

> *It is far easier for companies, managers, and systems when people keep their heads down and do the work.*

The kicker is this: We absorb that message to zip it long before we know we're absorbing it. We're taught in school to wait to be called on. Taught at home to be polite. Taught that drawing attention to ourselves is showing off. Taught that ambition is admirable in theory but frowned upon in practice.

> *By the time we reach adulthood, the pattern is set: We move through the world hoping our effort will "speak for*

**itself," all while forgetting that effort, by nature, has no
voice.**

Pillar 3 is about giving your effort a voice.

And despite what culture sometimes suggests, this isn't just a
female issue, though women do face specific structural barriers.
Men struggle with this, too. Many men have been socialized to
equate self-advocacy with ego, to believe that asking for support
or clarity makes them look weak, to rely on performance as proof
of competence. In fact, several studies show that both men and
women overestimate how negatively others will react when they
speak up for themselves. Psychologists call this the "self-advocacy
cost bias"—the belief that advocating for your work will backfire,
when in reality, most people respond positively to clarity and confidence.

The problem is not that people don't want to advocate. It's that
we've been trained not to.

Much of this struggle comes from what happens inside us long
before we ever open our mouths. We question whether we're ready.
We worry we'll seem too eager. We rehearse 30 versions of how to
phrase a sentiment and then never send the message. We convince
ourselves that the timing isn't quite right, that we need one more
year, one more project, one more certification, one more sign from
the universe before we feel good enough.

Now, let me hit you with this:

You're not waiting for more readiness.

You're waiting for permission.

Pillar 3 means reclaiming that permission.

The moment you stop assuming people know what you want and make your value visible, you've dipped a toe into self-advocacy. It's the courage to say, "I want this," not with entitlement, but with clarity.

It's time to refocus on actively shaping your career, rather than being carried by it. It's time to put into practice the radical belief that your voice deserves to be heard, not after you've achieved everything, but *as you build it.*

That is the heart of this pillar.

Not noise.

Not bravado.

Not competition.

Ownership.

Alignment.

Agency.

The Practice

If remembering who you are is the anchor, and finding your people is the circle around you, then speaking up is the bridge you build between your work and the world. Getting there is a practice, not a personality trait. You don't have to be loud, extroverted, fearless, or naturally charismatic. You just have to be willing.

For most people, the near-imperceptible change starts with noticing the tiny automatic ways you diminish your own contributions. How often do you say, "It was a team effort," when you were the one who salvaged the entire project at midnight? How often do you tell someone, "It was nothing," when it was, in fact, something? How often do you reel back your successes because you're afraid someone might think you're bragging?

Stop editing yourself out of your achievements! That is another part of self-advocacy.

You don't have to announce your accomplishments from the rooftops. Just stop erasing them.

Once you become aware of those micro-moments of living as less than, the practice becomes more intentional.

One of the simplest and most powerful tools I ever learned and still use constantly is the Rock Star List. I keep a folder in my inbox, and anytime someone sends me a compliment, shared praise, or points out a project that went well, I save it. Not because I need external validation, but because memory is unreliable. We forget what we've done. We forget how far we've come. We forget the impact we've made.

> *The Rock Star List becomes your evidence. Your grounding. Your reality check.*

Another practice you can use is what I call the Weekly Progress Ritual. At the end of each week, Friday afternoon, or Sunday night if that's your rhythm, take five minutes to write down what progressed. Not what was completed perfectly. Not what earned applause. Just what took you further.

This ritual trains your brain to recognize momentum, not perfection. Momentum gives you the language you need when someone asks, "What are you working on?" or "How's everything going?"

Instead of vague answers, you'll have substance to share. Clarity. Substance is confidence's closest friend.

Then comes the part that most people resist: Telling people what you want.

Not in a demanding way. Not as an ultimatum. But with the same elemental clarity you might've used years ago when you asked, "What will it take for me to get promoted?" That question was the earliest form of self-advocacy, even though you didn't know it at the time. Speaking up for yourself includes asking for direction, feedback, and opportunity so you can design your career on purpose.

Name your goals in the rooms where decisions are made. Mention a project you'd love to lead. Express curiosity about a skill you want to improve. Ask, "How can I prepare myself for X?" or "What would set me up for Y?" These strategic questions tell the people around you that you are not waiting passively; you are participating.

Research from organizational psychologist Dr. Laurie Weingart shows that self-advocacy is most effective when it is framed not as self-focus, but as alignment: "This is the impact I want to have. This is how I can contribute. This is where I see myself adding value next."

You're not asking for favors. You're articulating direction.

Speaking up is also about being authentically visible. Some people might share wins in team meetings. Others might offer a point of view in a discussion where they'd usually stay quiet. Still others might send a short note to a stakeholder summarizing progress. None of these requires bravado—only intention.

Intention might take the form of saying what you're scared to say out loud: "I'd like to be considered for that role." "I'd like to shadow that meeting." "I'd like to take lead on this initiative."

These sentences feel enormous the first time you say them, but they are the backbone of how careers ascend. They help the people who matter view you as someone others consider.

A practice many people overlook is the art of narrating their work transparently—not defensively. Instead of keeping your progress nestled away into a corner, let your leaders know what's happening *as* it happens. A simple message will suffice: "Just wanted to share that the pilot session landed well, with 95% engagement. Here's what participants loved, and here's what I'm adjusting for next time."

It's factual.

It's useful.

And it ensures no one is surprised when your name comes up.

Self-advocacy means making it clear when something *isn't* working. Reinforce those boundaries! Ask for clarity, and push back on unrealistic timelines. Try saying, "I need support with this." These are all forms of advocating for your success.

What Jenny Wood, *New York Times* #1 best-selling author of *Wild Courage: Go After What You Want and Get It*, calls "courageous honesty" is integrated in every form of self-advocacy. She writes about how the most transformative shifts often start with the smallest truths spoken at the right time. You're not issuing dramatic ultimatums. You're asking for correctness and speaking the truth that aligns you with who you want to become.

The final part of the practice does not get talked about enough: You don't need to feel ready to advocate for yourself. Do it while your voice is shaking.

Confidence doesn't come before advocacy. Confidence is the *result* of advocacy.

You learn your voice by using it.

You learn your value by naming it.

You learn your strength by stepping into it, not waiting for someone to invite you to see it.

Speaking up is not a personality trait. It is a habit you build consistently over time.

Like every meaningful practice, it starts with believing in and wanting a different reality, taking a single step, and accumulating new behaviors until eventually, it's how you move through the world.

The Barriers and Breakthroughs

For many of us, the earliest barrier of Pillar 3 is the belief that our work should speak for itself.

Psychologists call this pattern self-silencing. It happens when people minimize their contributions for fear of appearing arrogant or demanding. Dr. Dana Jack's decades of research on the topic prove that self-silencing has become so normalized that we barely recognize it as a behavior. It feels polite. It feels professional. It feels moral. Until the moment we realize it's also keeping us invisible.

There is an assumption that speaking up will backfire. That asking for a raise will make us seem entitled. That expressing ambition will make us look impatient. That sharing achievements will irritate people. This fear is wildly inaccurate.

Colleagues respond far more positively to self-advocacy than we predict. But the fear persists because it's formed not in logic but in emotion: the primal human need to belong. If we believe that speaking up risks rejection, our nervous system will try to protect us by choosing silence.

> *Then there's the barrier most people never name: We worry that advocating for ourselves will expose the possibility that we're not as capable as we hope.*

It's sometimes safer to hide behind effort instead of risking the vulnerability of saying out loud, "I want this." Once you name a desire, someone can say no. Silence protects you from that, and it also keeps you stuck.

> *Silence benefits the system. But it rarely benefits the individual.*

The good news, and this is where the breakthrough comes in, is that the moment you decide to advocate for yourself, your entire landscape stabilizes.

When you start speaking up, you experience what researchers call competence visibility: the psychological effect that happens when others can finally *see* your work that they've been relying on all along. People trust what they can observe. They support what they understand. They champion what they recognize. Self-advocacy is not demanding anything new of others; it is illuminating what was already there.

Maybe the best profound internal breakthrough is that *your nervous system recalibrates.* Advocacy activates brain regions associated with agency, self-efficacy, and motivation. When you name your worth, your mind believes it. When you express what you want, your body orients toward it.

Dr. Albert Bandura's research on self-efficacy shows that taking even the smallest act of agency strengthens your belief in your ability to influence your environment. That belief becomes a reinforcing spiral: The more you advocate, the more confident you feel; the more confident you feel, the more naturally you advocate.

Something else happens, too. You stop mistaking smallness for humility. You recognize that advocating for yourself is not competing with others; it's collaborating with your future. And when you are firmly entrenched in living as this new you, people respond differently to you. Not because you're louder, but because you're clearer. Self-advocacy creates opportunity where previously there was only assumption about your abilities.

Perhaps the most liberating part of practicing this pillar is that once you learn to speak up for yourself, you stop waiting for someone else to rescue your career. You stop hoping for recognition that may never come. You stop tying your worth to whether someone else sees it.

The barriers are real, but so is the transformation.

Cross this threshold even once, and you'll never again believe the lie that keeping your mouth shut keeps you safe.

Your Next Step

By now, you've likely realized that no matter how capable, loyal, collaborative, or hardworking you are, none of it replaces the moment you learn how to stand in your own voice.

Self-advocacy is a skill. And like any skill, it grows through deliberate, repeated action. It also unhooks your future from other people's timing.

Start to rewrite your career with clarity, not courage. Before you say anything out loud, articulate what you want privately.

Close the door.

Open a notebook.

Write the answers to these questions without editing:

1. *What opportunities do I want in the next 12 months?*

2. *How do I want to be seen?*

3. *What strengths do I want others to recognize in me?*

4. *What kind of work energizes me most?*

5. *What am I no longer willing to shrink or stay silent about?*

Next, prepare your advocacy anchors—the simple statements that make it easier to speak up without stumbling. Think of them as scripts for your nervous system.

Three anchors to try:

1. **The Clarity Anchor:**
    "One of the areas I'd really like to grow into is ..."

2. **The Contribution Anchor:**
   "Here's what I've delivered, and here's where I can add even greater value ..."

3. **The Visibility Anchor:**
   "I want to make sure you're aware of ..."

Your answers provide context. When you make leaders aware of what you really want, they can make better decisions because they'll finally have a full picture of who you are and what you can do.

Then, choose a low-stakes rep, your first small act of self-advocacy. Think of it like starting with a lighter weight: You're not trying to prove anything; you're just building the muscle.

Make it manageable and meaningful, so your nervous system won't interpret it as danger.

A few possibilities:

1. *Tell your manager one accomplishment you're proud of this quarter.*

2. *Ask to shadow a meeting, project, or task aligned with your goals.*

3. *Share a recent win in a team channel.*

4. *Request feedback with the intention of understanding, not defending, your strengths.*

5. *Volunteer a single idea or perspective in a meeting where you'd usually stay quiet.*

Next, schedule your values check-in, a five-minute weekly ritual.

Open your calendar and pick a recurring slot. Each week, at that time, ask yourself:

1. *Did I advocate for myself at least once?*

2. *Did I dim myself anywhere out of habit?*

3. *What is one moment next week where I can speak up with intention?*

Neuroscience confirms that repetition, not intensity, rewires behavior. This is how your new habit forms.

Self-advocacy does not happen in isolation; make sure to set yourself up with these guided tools to make the work easier and more structured.

Your next step is to take the How Invisible Are You at Work? Quiz at ChooseYouBook.com. Your personalized report includes: Micro-actions for being vocal suited to your specific archetype style, reflection prompts tailored to your blind spots, scripts and sentence starters for difficult conversations, strategies to increase visibility without forcing extroversion, and a roadmap instructing you in how to build momentum without burnout.

Don't get it twisted. It's not about becoming louder.

It's about becoming *heard.*

Once you know that, you can move on to the final step—the one most people skip:

Tell someone you trust what you're working on. According to the American Society of Training & Development, accountability increases your follow-through by up to 65%. You're not asking for permission. You're letting your voice exist outside your head. You're choosing to be witnessed in your effort.

You've spent long enough waiting to be tapped on the shoulder.

This is the moment you tap yourself.

And once you start, you'll never again forget what it feels like to use your voice on purpose.

Chapter 20:

Pillar 4—Start Before You're Ready

"Come Alive"
—The Greatest Showman Soundtrack

The Moment You Move Anyway

Pillar 4 marks the moment the dormant parts of you wake up, all because you dared to move before certainty arrived. Growth isn't organized or neat. Momentum isn't polite. But your life doesn't expand through contemplation alone.

You feel that? That's the energy rushing back into your system the moment you say yes to something that scares you just enough. That's your pulse rising. The thrill of reentering your life with both feet.

In this pillar, you come alive again.

For me, that moment began years before I ever realized I was living in motion instead of waiting.

During my master's program, we were given a list of 20 leadership books to choose from, a neat, structured menu of titles meant to shape our thinking about the future of work. I didn't recognize most of the authors, didn't research the companies they led, and I didn't analyze which book matched most closely with my career goals. I simply scanned the list, paused on one title, and leaned in.

The Heart of Business.

I chose that title the way a child chooses a seashell: instinctively, without overthinking, drawn in by a hunch I couldn't articulate. I had no idea who the author was. I didn't know he had led one of the most celebrated corporate turnarounds of our time. I didn't know he had redefined what modern leadership could look like. I didn't know this book—chosen on a whim—would become one of the binding properties of my professional life.

But as I turned the pages, I opened up and became receptive.

The way Hubert Joly wrote about leadership wasn't grand or performative. It was human. Grounded. Uncomfortably honest. It made me question every assumption I'd carried into the workplace. He didn't just talk about values; he lived them in the baser moments, in the decisions only he wrestled with, and in the board meetings that began with purpose that then filtered down to the people and ultimately profits. He was not living a slogan for attention; he was practicing it as a lived sequence because he believed in it. Because it was a value.

Each chapter was a recalibration.

Each story was permission.

Each principle whispered, *This is what leadership could be.*

I remember closing the book one night and saying out loud, to no one, "Imagine having that kind of impact."

The sentence as it burst out of me was surprising. It was bigger than me, like it belonged to someone braver, who was already standing on a stage I hadn't yet built. I filed the thought away, as we do with desires that seem too audacious to claim.

Fast forward to writing this book.

I kept thinking about Joly's work. His approach. His belief in the humanity inside organizations and the potential inside people. And somewhere between writing about courage and invisibility and agency, a thought surfaced that made my stomach churn.

Ask him to be part of this book.

Immediately, my inner dialogue revolted.

Absolutely not.

You can't email him.

He doesn't know you.

Stay in your lane.

Be realistic.

Don't embarrass yourself.

The fear came fast and familiar, with a surging rush of reasons elucidating why the idea was ridiculous. I could practically feel my nervous system searching for the exit ramp.

But underneath the noise was a persistent, irritatingly steady voice.

What if you try?

What if readiness isn't the point?

What if this is your come-alive moment, the exact kind of leap you're writing about?

The contradiction was maddening. My fear wanted safety. My intuition wanted expansion. Then, it struck me: This is what "Start before you're ready" looks like in real time.

It's not glamorous, confident, or Hollywood-inspiring. It's actually rather anticlimactic—just a woman staring at her laptop, arguing with herself.

I wrote that email to Joly the way you walk onto a stage you're not sure you belong on, heart first, knees slightly shaking. I told him the truth: that his book had shaped me, that his leadership had redefined how I thought about impact, and that his work was part of the reason I had the courage to write my book. I didn't try to sound impressive. I didn't pretend to be more established than I was. I wrote it the way I would write to someone I admired deeply, even if he never saw it.

Then, with my whole body buzzing, I hit "Send."

What happened next is the part I still can't recount without shaking my head at the absurd, stunning magic of it:

He said yes.

Hubert Joly, the CEO whose book cracked something open in me, the leader I had studied, the voice that has shaped so much of my journey since, said yes. To me. To this book.

To being part of something I used to believe I had no right to ask for.

That was when I understood the power of moving before you feel ready. The way one trembling yes can rewrite your entire understanding of what's possible.

And it didn't stop there.

Emboldened by that one yes, I reached out to two other CEOs I admire. Their replies are still floating around somewhere in the universe. Maybe they'll respond. Maybe they won't. That's not the point.

The point is this:

You don't need every yes. You just need the right one, the one that reinforces the version of you who can send the next email.

This is the advent of your next chapter—that takes place between fear and action.

Where readiness has not yet arrived, but courage has already started clearing a path—that, *that* is the moment you *come alive.*

What Pillar 4 Really Means

Starting before you're ready isn't about leaping without looking or pretending the fear isn't there. It's about understanding that waiting for readiness is one of the most effective ways to keep your life exactly as it is.

Albert Bandura's research on self-efficacy shows that nothing builds confidence more reliably than "mastery experiences," the moments when you attempt an aim before you feel qualified and discover, through action, that you're more capable than you assumed.

Translated: Waiting to feel ready doesn't move you closer to courage; it moves you deeper into hesitation.

Pillar 4 asks for a different relationship with fear. Not to ignore it, overpower it, or "Fake it till you make it," but to interpret it correctly. Fear isn't always a warning. Often, it's information. It tells you that you are touching the edges of your current identity. It tells you that you're standing at the border between who you've been and who you're becoming. The presence of fear doesn't mean stop. It means pay attention, because a meaningful moment is happening.

Researchers Katy Milkman and Teresa Amabile have shown that humans are far more capable of rapid learning, context adaptation, and responsibility-taking than we predict. But those capacities activate only *after* we leap, not before. Readiness is backward-looking. Growth is forward-moving.

Then there's the truth most of us know on some level but rarely say out loud:

Sometimes "I'm not ready yet" is a socially acceptable disguise for "I'm afraid of what this might require of me."

Beginning asks you to risk visibility. To be seen trying. To be seen not fully formed. It asks you to tolerate the discomfort of being a beginner again. It asks you to step into rooms you're not sure you belong in and trust that you'll learn the gist of them once you're inside.

Starting before you're ready doesn't mean you're reckless. It relies on your self-trust.

What feels like jumping the gun is really you deciding to put faith into your ability to learn more, rather than focusing on your desire to control the outcome.

It's the willingness to take the step without every detail being exact or even known.

It's the understanding that momentum creates clarity far faster than contemplation ever will.

Maybe, most importantly, it's choosing participation over perfection.

This fourth pillar dismantles the quiet lie that has held so many of us back: the belief that only the "fully formed" version of you deserves to embark on anything new. Stop waiting for that version, because that's not the one you want to unleash. You want the one who emerges *after* that—you want the *you* version of you.

This pillar is an embodied decision, tethered to all the connective tissue of the new you. It says: "I can begin, even here. Even now. Even in uncertainty."

The Practice

If you imagine this pillar as a thunderclap of bravery, you're missing the truth: Most turning points begin as minuscule interruptions to your life's familiar rhythm. A turning point might be defined by a moment of curiosity or a sentence you've recorded, even though you're not sure why. It might manifest as a thought you don't dismiss *this time*.

For many people, the practice begins when you decide to stop obeying and start observing, when you notice the exact moment your instinct is to downplay yourself.

What if you allowed your instinct to retreat to become a signal?

Not a stop sign.

A doorway.

Behavioral science calls this cognitive reframing, and it refers to what happens when you move from interpreting discomfort as danger to interpreting it as growth-in-progress. You don't have to override the fear. You just have to reinterpret the meaning you've attached to it.

One of the simplest practices you can apply right now to overcome your fear is the 10-Second Rule:

When fear tells you to wait, buy yourself 10 seconds of courage.

Just 10.

Most of the time, readiness never arrives, but courage often appears in a thin slice of time when you let your body act before your fear has a chance to reframe the story.

Another essential part of this practice is what psychologists call exposure to possibility, or intentionally placing yourself near what you desire, even if you don't feel prepared to claim it yet. This might mean attending an event where you feel slightly out of your depth, applying for a role you're not 100% qualified for, or scheduling a call with someone whose career is two steps ahead of yours. This research from Stanford's Behavior Design Lab shows that proximity changes belief. Being near what you want recalibrates your understanding of what is possible for you.

Contrary to how we romanticize it, momentum is rarely loud. It often begins with administrative tasks: opening a document, booking a slot on your calendar, outlining a rough draft, or gathering the first two resources you'll need for a project. Neuroscience tells us that action reduces anxiety, not the other way around. Once your brain sees movement, it releases dopamine, not because the goal has been achieved, but because you have engaged the system.

It's not the size of the step.

It's the direction.

A practice I often recommend to gain traction is the "Embarrassingly Early Draft." You can use it for more than writing ideas, pitches, proposals, projects, or any initiative where you are still stuck at the starting line. In essence, you'll create a messy, honest first version before your perfectionism has time to insert self-doubt.

Another powerful tool is the "Future Self Anchor." Research by Dr. Hal Hershfield shows that when people vividly imagine their future selves, they make braver decisions in the present. Try repeatedly to envision the version of you who already took the leap. What room is she in? How does he speak? What decision did she make that this moment is asking for? That version of you becomes a guide, not a fantasy.

And finally, there's one practice that matters more than all the others: letting yourself be witnessed. Not by everyone. Not by the internet. By one person you trust, someone who supports who you are becoming and has the kind of presence that makes you sit up a little straighter. It could be a mentor you respect, a colleague who gets it, your partner, or that one friend who doesn't let you wriggle out of your own potential.

Tell them plainly what you're starting. Tell them the part you don't want to admit, to: "I'm scared. My voice is shaky. I'm doing it anyway." You might feel the urge to soften it, to laugh it off, to say, "It's not a big deal," even when it is. Don't. Say it out loud.

Research on goal sharing suggests this matters, but not in a cheesy "accountability buddy" way. It works because the right person can support you, remind you, encourage you, and help you keep the goal on your radar when life interferes. And if the person is someone whose opinion you genuinely value, their witness can sharpen your commitment, not through pressure, but through a quiet internal shift: *I said I'm doing this. I meant it.* You stop carrying the beginning alone. You stop trying to be brave in private. Let someone be in it with you.

The Barriers and Breakthroughs

For every person who dreams of being different and more relevant to themselves, thousands never do take that shot, not because they lack skill or desire, but because their feet are cemented to the familiar. Starting before you're ready sounds empowering in theory, but in practice, it requires you to walk straight into the places your nervous system has spent years trying to avoid.

One barrier is what psychologists call the readiness fallacy; it's the belief that confidence must arrive before action. It's a myth rooted in how we're socialized: Don't attempt something until you're certain you'll succeed, until you've mastered every detail, until you can guarantee the outcome. Readiness becomes a delay tactic disguised as responsibility. You tell yourself you're not avoiding the leap, you're preparing for it. But preparation without action is just prolonged hesitation.

The next barrier is catastrophic forecasting—the brain's unfortunate talent for imagining every possible tragic scenario for whatever you are undertaking. Neuroscience tells us the brain is wired for survival, not success, which means it instinctively amplifies the risk of trying, so it feels unsafe, and minimizes the risk of staying still. That fear isn't irrational. It's outdated. Your brain is protecting a primitive version of you, one who didn't have the tools you have now.

Another subtler barrier is identity inertia, the quiet belief that you are only allowed to pursue the life that matches who you've been, not who you want to become. That voice shows up as:

Who do you think you are?

Other people do that, not you.

Stay in your lane.

> **This voice lives in the background and is rarely loud enough to be challenged; it influences decisions so subtly that you don't realize how many opportunities you've talked yourself out of.**

And perhaps the most painful barrier of all is what I call impostor anticipation, not impostor syndrome itself. I mean the expectation that if you start down a new path, someone will eventually expose you. This fear halts people before they ever start. If you never step into the arena, no one can question your place in it. Safety masquerades as self-preservation, when in reality it's self-abandonment.

Most people only ever feel the fear. They never stay long enough to experience what comes next: the shift. But you should know that every one of those barriers grows more conquerable the moment you take even the smallest action. Not because fear disappears, but because action gives your brain new data to work with.

When you try, even imperfectly, your nervous system recalibrates. The mind that once insisted *This will destroy you* suddenly has to contend with the fact that you are still standing. The voice that warned, *Everyone will think you don't belong,* is forced to acknowledge that no one noticed the wobble except you. Even the old narrative of *You'll embarrass yourself* loses its edge when the only evidence available is that you handled the moment with more adeptness than you expected.

Psychologists call this a corrective experience; it's the moment lived reality disproves the story fear has been rehashing for years. You might think that you need a hundred corrective experiences. Actually, you just need one. One email sent. One risk taken. One room entered. One conversation initiated. One step that proves, undeniably, that you can be scared and skillful at the same time is all it takes to create the first dent in fear's credibility.

From there, something almost undetectable but deeply powerful happens. Momentum forms.

Starting before you're ready changes how you respond to fear. Doubt no longer dictates your decisions because you no longer wait for certainty before you act. Perfectionism quiets once you're actually doing the thing. When you're in it, there's no luxury of over-analyzing whether you're ready or worthy or impressive enough. You're too busy paying attention to what's in front of you. The question stops being *Do I feel confident?* and becomes something more practical: *Can I stay with this long enough to learn?*

Most people wait for permission to try, to fail, to start, to begin badly and bravely. The turning point comes when you realize the permission you've been hoping for will not come from a manager, a mentor, a title, a sign, or the universe. It will come from *you.*

Your Next Step

You're ready. You may not feel polished, fearless, or perfectly prepared, but it's still time to honor both your courage and your capacity by taking the following steps:

1. Rely on clarity, not bravado.

Before you take action, make sure the real version of you knows what you want. Close your door, open a notebook, and write down the opportunities, experiences, and changes you value. You're not making a five-year plan; you're charting your trajectory. This isn't manifestation. It's cognitive anchoring.

Let it be honest. Let it be audacious. Let yourself admit what you've pretended not to want.

2. Take the smallest step of the real action.

People often assume that you have to take a monstrous lurch forward to make a difference. You don't. You just need to be willing to walk through a door. Behavioral science calls this a *minimum viable step*, but it still counts as progress. For you, it might be drafting an email or registering for a workshop.

Again, the size of the step doesn't matter.

The direction does.

3. Create your "future evidence" list.

Document what you are doing as you do it, and do not wait for it to feel impressive. This list is not for milestones or highlight moments. It is for the small ordinary actions you usually dismiss, the early alarm you didn't snooze, the uncomfortable conversation you didn't avoid, the first messy attempt you almost talked yourself out of. Each step, each try, each choice to move instead of hesitate becomes evidence, not for the world, but for you.

4. Bring one trusted person into your beginning.

Accountability equals being witnessed. Choose one person, not the brashest in your circle, not the harshest critic, but someone who generously supports your ambition. Tell them the truth: that you're embracing a new opportunity, that it scares you a little, and that you don't want to do it in isolation.

Letting them see you strengthens your follow-through more than any other productivity strategy will.

5. Commit to a 24-hour action window.

Momentum dissolves when you give fear too much time. Choose one meaningful action you can complete within the next day; make it clear, feasible, and undeniably forward. Think of this step as lighting the fuse. You don't have to build the fireworks display. You just have to ignite it.

When you do, your nervous system receives a new message: *I can move even when I'm not comfortable.* Every bold step you take after that will only add to the foundation, enabling another bolder action.

6. Track your progress in a way your future self will thank you for.

Once a week, take five minutes to reflect:

1. *What did I do this week that the previous version of me wouldn't have attempted?*

2.   *What fear shrank because I acted?*

3.   *What opened, internally or externally, because I started?*

Repetition rewires readiness. This ritual is the rewiring.

7. Let the structure support you.

Your How Invisible Are You at Work? Quiz from ChooseYouBook. com includes practical, tailored tools to help you build momentum without burning out, micro-actions calibrated to your archetype, scripts for difficult conversations, and visibility techniques that don't require extroversion.

Readiness is not the doorway. Movement is.

And each time you move, even by an inch, you can build the evidence to trust yourself with the next step and the next and the next.

Your life expands not when you finally stop feeling afraid, but when you ultimately stop letting fear decide the timeline.

This is the beginning of your beginning.

Your only job now is simple.

Move.

Chapter 21:

Pillar 5—Reset Your Perspective

"Rewrite the Stars"
—The Greatest Showman Soundtrack

The Moment You See the Ceiling Was Self-Installed

Every real transformation that rearranges the way you move through the world can be boiled down to perspective. I don't mean the circumstances around you, but the framework through which you interpret your experiences. So many of the ceilings we consider immovable aren't imposed by the world; they've been installed by the stories we've rehearsed about who we're allowed to be.

This truth didn't land for me during a crisis or a dramatic turning point. It came while listening to an audiobook I picked up on a whim: *No B.S. Marketing to the Affluent* by Dan S. Kennedy.

Not exactly the kind of book you'd expect to spark an existential shift.

I thought I was going to learn about audience segmentation or buying behaviors; maybe I'd discover a clever hack I could apply to my business. Instead, I found myself staring at a statistic that made everything inside me crash to a halt:

The majority of millionaires are self-made.

Depending on the study we're talking about, the range runs from roughly 60% to 80%. These people aren't trust-fund inheritors, they don't come from generational wealth, nor were they "chosen from birth." They are all self-made.

At first, I just blinked when I heard those blaring facts. My brain did that stutter it does when information doesn't fit my worldview. Then the challenging inner voice came, the one that always arrives before I'm ready for it:

If most people who have achieved extraordinary things started from ordinary places … then what exactly separates them from me?

This question landed with uncomfortable, honest accuracy. I started thinking about the people whose stories have inspired me: Sarah Blakely cutting the feet off her pantyhose in a tiny apartment, pitching an idea no one believed in except her. Gary Vaynerchuk building businesses long before anyone christened him a visionary. Oprah refusing to let her early circumstances dictate her future. Steve Jobs hunting down parts and believers, turning a garage project into a company before anyone took him seriously.

None of them was handed permission.

None of them waited for a perfect moment.

None of them treated the limits in front of them as fixed.

Their backgrounds weren't extraordinary. Their perspectives were.

As I listened to the audiobook, something in me paused. I rewound the section and listened again because the recognition landed harder the second time. If I'm being brutally honest, the gap between the people who had accomplished so much and me wasn't defined by talent, potential, or intelligence. It was the belief in what was possible, what was available, and what could be rewritten.

At first, I didn't even plan to include this as a pillar in the book. I thought the other four were enough: Remember Who You Are, Find Your People, Speak Up, and Start Before You're Ready. But as I kept writing, it became obvious: Without a perspective big enough to hold who you're becoming, every other pillar collapses.

Insignificant vision shrinks your courage.

A fixed perspective shrinks your opportunities.

A limited belief shrinks your entire life.

Resetting your perspective can open up new worlds to you, not because your existence suddenly becomes limitless, but because you stop accepting the limits you assumed were permanent.

Get to this stage, and you can stop living as a witness to your life and start participating in the creation of it.

Before you know it, you'll be rewriting the stars.

What Pillar 5 Really Means

Resetting your perspective doesn't refer to unquestioned optimism or "thinking positively." It's more about recognizing how your inner narrative has been deciding what's possible for you, often without your consent.

Here's how we grow into bystanders in our own lives: From an early age, you internalize messages about who you are and where you belong. Some come from family: "*Be realistic. Don't reach too high.*" Some come from culture: "*People like you don't end up in those rooms.*" Some come from workplaces that reward predictability over imagination: "*This is how we've always done it,*" or "*That's above your pay grade.*" Over time, these messages harden into an unwritten rulebook that's strong enough to shape every decision you make.

Perspective is powerful precisely because it operates in the background. It determines the risks you take, the ceilings you refuse to test, and the invitations you assume are meant for other people. It decides whether you interpret a setback as proof you should slink away or as data you can grow from. It colors your view of opportunity as scarce and reserved for a chosen few or as available and movable if you're willing to participate in it.

That's why the stories of people like Sarah Blakely, Gary Vaynerchuk, Oprah, Steve Jobs, and countless others matter here, not as "success porn," but as evidence. Their origin stories aren't tied up in a bow. They're full of rejection, uncertainty, and improvisation. They're not a different species from you. They started simply and with an ingrained decision: "*My starting point is not my ceiling.*"

- Sarah Blakely talks about being raised to treat failure as information instead of shame.

- Gary Vee speaks about his immigrant upbringing and the mindset that nothing is predetermined.

- Oprah built an entire career on the conviction that her circumstances could shape her but not chain her.

- Steve Jobs famously reminded us that "Everything around you that you call life was made up by people that were no smarter than you."

Their lives are not blueprints for you to copy. They are reminders that the limits we perceive are often cultural stories, not actual constraints.

> *Resetting your perspective requires stepping back far enough to see which stories you've been living inside— stories about worth, capability, timing, ambition, identity, and belonging.*

Here is the heart of this pillar:

Your circumstances don't determine your horizon.

Your perspective does.

Perspective widens the path.

Perspective changes what you believe is available to you.

Perspective transforms possibility from theory into direction.

This fifth pillar doesn't ask you to ignore reality.

It asks you to stop being unnecessarily limited by it.

The Practice

Don't expect a one-time epiphany when you reset your perspective. Do realize that it's a practice concerning how you think, interpret, and respond to your life in real time.

Train yourself to notice the moment your thinking narrows. Does this sound familiar? You receive feedback and immediately hear that inner voice: *I'm not cut out for this.* A project stalls, and your brain jumps to: *See? I knew this was too big for me.* Someone else gets an opportunity you wanted, and the story becomes: *People like me never get picked.* Those thoughts may feel factual, but they're mere interpretations. The first step in this practice is catching them the second you can hear them in your mind.

When you notice a familiar, limiting script, pause long enough to name it:

This is the story where I assume I'm behind.

This is the story where I decide I'm not that kind of person.

This is the story where I treat one event as permanent proof.

Naming the story separates you from it. Now it's not *the truth*; it's a *version* of the truth.

> **From there, practice asking a better question. Instead of "What's wrong with me?" try "What else might be true here?" Instead of "Why can't I do this?" try "What would Future Me see if they looked back at this moment?"**

That single tactic pulls you out of tunnel vision and into a wider view. Cognitive science shows that the questions you ask literally direct what your brain pays attention to.

Another part of the practice is deliberate reframing: not pretending that everything is fine, but choosing a lens to peer through that keeps you moving forward.

"I failed" becomes "I learned where my limits are today."

"I'm behind everyone else" becomes "I'm earlier in my story than I thought."

"I'm not that person" becomes "I haven't become that person *yet*."

Over time, these reframes train your mind to see movement instead of dead ends.

You can also reset perspective by zooming out. When you encounter a defining moment, ask, "How will this look in three years? Or five years?" Many experiences that feel catastrophic at the time they happen can dramatically diminish in intensity when placed on a longer timeline. You're not dismissing the feelings; you're putting them in proportion.

Once you've mastered this thought reset, build non-intimidating experiments into your week that challenge your assumptions. If you've been telling yourself, "I could never speak in front of a group," volunteer to share an update in an intimate meeting. If you've believed, "I'm not the type of person who networks," send one genuine message to someone you respect. The point is not the outcome; it's to give your brain new evidence: *I can do things the old story said I couldn't.*

Finally, notice what you consume. Perspective is porous. The accounts you follow, the conversations you stay in, and the content you watch all contribute to how you see yourself. Curate your inputs as if you are protecting a long-term investment. Spend more time listening to people who stretch your sense of what's possible and less time marinating in voices that confirm your underachieving fears.

Resetting your perspective doesn't mean you've suddenly become limitless. You're simply refusing to live as if you're trapped—because you're not.

The Barriers and Breakthroughs

One of the biggest barriers to resetting your perspective is how quietly your worldview shrinks. No alarm goes off the moment you stop imagining more for yourself. Your perspective contracts through routines, obligations, the sheer busyness of staying afloat, and the circles you move in. If you stay on this road, before long, the boundaries of your thinking will match the boundaries of your calendar; you may mistake familiarity for truth.

Psychologists call this cognitive tunneling: meaning your focus narrows so much that you stop perceiving alternate paths, even when they're right there. Opportunity is not disappearing. Your mind has just stopped recognizing it as something that belongs to you.

A more modern barrier is possibility blindness. When you've lived for years with financial, structural, and emotional constraints, your brain adapts to anticipate limitations. It ceases scanning for what could be different. You don't ask and have no curiosity about any other alternative because you've already rehearsed the "no" in your mind. You don't imagine yourself in certain roles because your internal casting director never puts your name forward.

And then there is the emotional resistance that might be the most human barrier of all: The discomfort of realizing that, if more is possible, then you might have been living beneath your potential for a while. That thought can sting.

**It's easier, sometimes, to stay inside the myth that says,
This is just how life is *than to confront the vulnerability
of* Maybe I've underestimated myself.**

Still, you'll want to keep pressing because this is exactly how the breakthrough happens.

You'll know you're working it when you start to think: *What if this limit isn't actually fixed?* When you hear the origin story of someone you admire, and instead of feeling distance, you feel resonance. When you think, *If they could rewrite their story, maybe I can, too,* and a crack appears in the framework that's kept you contained.

Neuroplasticity research documents that when you disrupt old patterns of thought, even slightly, new neural pathways form. That means each time you challenge a belief like "I can't" or "not for me" and choose a different response, you are physically rewiring the way your brain understands possibility. What once felt impossible becomes conceivable. What once felt out of reach becomes a stretch instead of a fantasy.

Finally, perspective doesn't just change how you *feel* about your life. It changes what you believe is legitimately available to you. When you swap in a new lens to zoom in on the real view of who you are and what you're capable of, you can stop confusing your starting point with your potential. You can stop treating other people's paths as proof of your limits. You can stop assuming the script is already written.

Perspective is the power that turns "unlikely" into "why not?" and "not me" into "maybe me" then eventually into "of course, me."

Your Next Step

Resetting your perspective doesn't require a grand reinvention.

Get curious about what you can achieve. Don't worry about certainty right now. Just take a quiet moment this week during a coffee break, before bed, or between meetings, and write down the assumptions you've been carrying as truth. For instance:

I'm not senior enough yet.

People like me don't end up in those roles.

I can't charge that much.

I'm not the visionary type.

I need one more degree before I'm taken seriously.

Seeing these beliefs on paper powerfully externalizes them, allowing you to explore them instead of taking them as facts. And you'll want to do this because once you've named a belief, your mind can observe it rather than automatically obey it.

Next, borrow a perspective bigger than your own. Choose three people whose stories remind you that extraordinary lives rarely begin with extraordinary circumstances.

I look up to Sarah Blakely, with her $5,000 in savings and door-to-door fax machine sales; Oprah, who transformed profound adversity into an empire; Steve Jobs, experimenting in a garage; Gary Vaynerchuk, who didn't look like the "type" of entrepreneur anyone would bet on, yet he built anyway.

Spend 10 minutes reading or watching about their beginnings, not their highlight reels. When you see how ordinary their starting points were, your brain can loosen its grip on "not me."

Then complete a Perspective Stretch. Take the dream you've filed under "unrealistic," and write down what a version of it five times smaller could look like. If the dream is writing a book, the stretch might be drafting one article or one messy chapter. If the dream is starting a business, the stretch might be outlining a simple offer or having one conversation with a potential client. You're not minimizing the dream. You're changing the scale of your first step so your nervous system can tolerate it.

With these new ways of looking at your world in place, you can realign your environment with the future you're stepping into. Follow one new voice on LinkedIn whose thinking challenges your default lens. Listen to a podcast or talk by someone whose life looks nothing like your current reality but everything like your future one.

In one conversation this week, choose a real moment of friction, and instead of assuming your perspective is the only valid one, ask someone you trust, "*How would you approach this?*" Then listen without defending your original plan. Perspective grows through proximity, through letting your thinking brush up against someone else's.

> **Once you feel ready, take a single concrete action that aligns with the expanded version of yourself.**

Email someone who intimidates you. Apply for an opportunity you don't feel fully ready for. Pitch the idea you've been editing in your head. That action isn't just about outcomes; it sends the message to your mind: *I see myself differently now.*

Finally, reflect on your new perspective. At the end of the week, sit with this question:

"Where did I assume the ceiling was when, in reality, I was only touching the one I built?"

Let whatever answers come, come. You're not judging yourself; you're noticing where your perspective has been smaller than your potential. Do this enough, and over time, this new framing becomes a habit, a way of seeing the world that refuses to default to smallness.

And if you want guidance as you do this work, go to ChooseYou-Book.com and complete the How Invisible Are You at Work? Quiz. Your personalized report includes visibility strategies, mindset shifts, identity-expansion prompts, and tools to help you step into a version of yourself whose perspective is no longer inherited or limited, but chosen.

Pillar 5 ultimately teaches you that your life expands or contracts based on the lens you choose to look through.

Once you've seen the shortcomings of that lens, you can choose a wider one, one that makes more of your life possible.

Chapter 22:

The Life You're Stepping Back Into

"It's My Life"
—Bon Jovi

There's a moment at the end of any period of self-work where you look up and realize you've been changing in real time, without waiting for permission or applause.

Maybe you said no to something you once accepted out of habit.

Maybe you stopped apologizing for taking up half a chair, half a breath, half a sentence.

Maybe you closed your laptop before exhaustion pried it from your hands.

Individually, these moments look ordinary. Together, they are the first signs that you have begun choosing yourself.

That's why this chapter opens with "It's My Life," a song that doesn't ask for approval or wait for conditions to improve. It's a declaration.

A line in the sand. A reminder that choosing yourself isn't loud or performative, but it is final.

And not because the world suddenly made it safe, but because *you finally decided to stop living on the outer perimeter of your own life.* That is the revolution this part of the book is guiding you toward.

What This Work Has Actually Built in You

Across the **5 Pillars of Agency**, you've done much more than reflect on ideas. You've practiced returning to yourself, steadily, imperfectly, and with more courage than you probably give yourself credit for.

You've remembered who you are and uncluttered your inner landscape enough to hear your voice without the noise of everyone else's expectations.

You've found your people, or at least allowed yourself to admit who feels like home and who requires you to be all you don't want to be.

You've begun to speak up, not to shout, but to match your outer voice to the weight of what you actually contribute.

You've moved before you felt ready, proving that readiness is a feeling that follows action, not a prerequisite for it.

You've reset your perspective, pulling apart the beliefs that have molded you while deciding which ones still deserve to stay.

These aren't isolated lessons. They work as a cycle you'll return to again and again. You remember, then reach, then speak, then move, then see differently. And then, because life is alive and demanding, you begin again. Each loop brings you closer to yourself, not further away.

The point isn't to master the pillars like a curriculum. Carry them lightly, the way you do with truths you no longer need to argue yourself into—those truths that become part of the architecture of how you live, how you choose, and how you step forward.

What Happens When You Step Back Into Your Life?

If you're waiting to feel transformed before you act differently, you'll wait forever. Transformation is catching the old patterns in motion and deciding mid-sentence, mid-email, mid-thought that you're not taking particular action anymore.

You will still slip into invisibility sometimes. You will still over-commit, retreat, hush your own ideas, or compare your internal knowing to someone else's curated highlight reel. But the difference now is that you'll *notice* the slips. Awareness is the first interruption. Choice is the second.

Now, you can no longer disappear accidentally.

That alone changes the path beneath your feet.

If you remember nothing else, remember this:

> ***You do not owe anyone the version of you that survived lesser seasons.***

You are allowed to outgrow what once felt safe. You are allowed to take up more space than people are used to giving you. You are allowed to be seen.

What You've Proven, Even If You Don't Feel It Yet

By reading this far and staying with ideas that likely touched tender, long-avoided places in your life, you've proven something essential: You are capable of showing up for yourself in ways you once believed were reserved for other people. You have already chosen yourself in ways that matter more than you realize.

Before You Turn the Page

You deserve tools that walk with you, not just ideas that fade when life gets shaky again. That's why I created the How Invisible Are You at Work? Quiz and the personalized report at ChooseYouBook. com to be a companion for this leg of your journey. When you feel yourself reverting to old patterns, let it remind you of where to begin again.

After all that, take a breath. You immersed yourself in some pretty deep work. Now, let the full scope of these pillars settle in your system. Let the work you've done here mean something.

You're not crossing into a new self.

You're reuniting with the person you were always meant to be.

From here, the rest of your life becomes not just a trial of endurance or navigation ...

With the tools you have learned in these pages, you can now participate fully in the life you want to lead, with a voice that finally sounds like your own.

> ***Nothing will change because you read this book.***
> ***Everything can change if you use it.***

Invisibility doesn't leave on its own. It leaves when you do something about it.

You didn't read this book because everything was fine. You read it because you're ready for more than "fine."

So, as you close these pages, don't close the conversation with yourself.

Choose one thing.

One boundary.

One conversation.

One step.

Say yes to your new life:

"I am here."

"I am not disappearing."

"I choose me."

And then, tomorrow, choose yourself again.

Acknowledgments

Darryl. This has been a wild, beautiful ride. From kids to moves, careers to businesses, from moments where the world felt steady to moments where it felt like everything around us was falling apart, we have kept choosing each other and building anyway. Hand in hand, heart to heart, we've made something strong and real, and I love the life we're creating, the incredible humans we're raising, and the dreams we keep building together. I don't know what's ahead, but I know this much: whatever comes, we stand firm, we keep going, and nothing gets in our way.

My children. Tristan, your heart is the most wonderful thing about you. You've checked in on this book more times than anyone, asked how it was going, noticed when I looked tired, and offered encouragement without being asked. Your kindness, warmth, and steady presence already make the world better. One day, whatever you choose to create, build, or engineer will leave humans better off because of you. I am endlessly honored to be your mom. Hayley, you bring the sunshine. Every note, every whiteboard message that says "You can do it because I love you" lives with me. Your joy is magnetic, your spirit is pure, and the way you show up lights up every room you enter. I am one lucky human to be your mom.

My dad. I wish you were here to see this. You always warned me about burning the candle at both ends, "Little Chicken," but I know you were cheering me on the whole time. Thank you for the Shania Twain nights, for the many moments you could have scolded me but chose not to, for bailing me out of countless flat tyres (honestly, why were there so many?), and for arriving at my house for a "quick cofs" that was never quick. I miss you every single day, my

Fashie Pashie. Thank you for knowing me, loving me, backing me, and seeing me for exactly who I am.

My mom. This book exists because you made sure it could. You carried responsibility with determination and stayed committed to what you believed mattered most. I grew up learning what commitment looks like, how much one person can carry, and what it means to keep going even when it isn't easy. Thank you for backing this book into the world and for the deep love and sense of responsibility that guided the choices you made. Those choices helped shape the woman who wrote this.

My siblings. We live far apart, and I miss you terribly, but when we're together, it's actual magic.

To my sister, Jenny, thank you for going first, always. You moved overseas as a mom with tiny babies and lit the path for me to follow. You remain my guiding light.

To my big brother, Gavin, thank you for making me slightly more cool and for your unwavering support as I've built my business and written this book. Your check-ins have meant more than you know.

And to my younger brother, Kevin. From nearly killing each other as kids, to jolling with fake IDs, to you showing up when I needed you most, to constantly helping me think bigger and better. You are my rock.

Robbie, Jeanne, and Taryn. Being part of your family has been one of the great joys of my life. I may not have been the obvious choice at first, especially given that I'd never even seen a cow up close, but you expanded my world in ways I'll always be grateful for. Jeanne, I treasure our chats. And Robbie, we still mourn your passing, but so you know, I drank a Windhoek just for you.

Peter and Claire. Twenty years of shared history is no small thing. Businesses built, risks taken, oceans crossed. We didn't just move to America at the same time, we moved our lives and our futures alongside each other. You understand the full arc of this journey because you've been living your own version of it right beside us. There is something rare about building a life in parallel with people who see it all unfold. Thank you for walking this road with us, for the loyalty, the laughter, the shared history, and for making a foreign place feel like home.

Tara Rynders. My muse. One of the very few humans with whom I feel genuinely celebrated. You care deeply, openly, and without condition. You meet life with open arms and an even more open heart. I want to learn from you, spend more time with you, and soak up your goodness whenever I can.

Kat Higgins. My person. The one I call at my lowest lows and my highest highs. The voice note recipient when I can barely breathe through tears, and the first call when something good happens. Even writing this makes me emotional. You are home.

Michelle Tucker. My ride or die. You've lived every stage of my life with me. If you ever start telling our secrets … well, I know a field. But truly, you are the sun to my sun, the fun to my fun, the sparkle to my sparkle.

Markus Bernhardt. One of the newest names here and one of the most impactful. Your unwavering support, thoughtful challenges, guidance, and well-timed call-outs have shaped this work more than I can fully express. Working with you has been a privilege, and I hope one day we'll read this together and smile at how far we've come since publication.

Coenie Kleinhans. Thank you for bringing my wacky ideas to life and for creating a cover that feels like this book before a single word is read. For over a decade, I've sent you half-formed thoughts, vague explanations, and sometimes barely that, and you've consistently turned them into masterpieces. You get me, and that makes the work feel light and joyful.

To the leaders who shaped me. Sashir Milne, you saw my potential long before I could. You didn't lead gently, but you led intentionally, with a shove in exactly the right direction. I moved faster and achieved more because of you. Travis Ketchel, even though our time working together was brief, your calm, thoughtful leadership left a lasting imprint. You showed me what grounded, mission-driven leadership can look like.

To the people who supported me with nothing to gain. Andy Storch, Yogi Mueller, Nigel Paine, Chris Taylor, Julie Dirksen, Sheridan Webb, Alaina Szlachta, Christopher Lind, Kelsea Warren, Andrew Barry, and Elena Agaragimova. Your generosity, insight, and encouragement mattered more than you know.

To the leaders who shaped my thinking and worldview. Brené Brown, Sarah Blakely, Hubert Joly, Steven Bartlett, and Jenny Wood. Your work challenges me, stretches me, and helps me see what's possible.

And finally, **Hilary Jastram**, my editor and publisher. What a joy you have been. You encouraged me, steadied me, let me fly, and hyped me up daily. This book is bold, brave, and unapologetic because of you. Thank you. Thank you. A hundred times, thank you.

Bibliography

Amabile, Teresa M., and Kramer, Steve J. *The Progress Principle: Using Small Wins to Ignite Joy, Engagement, and Creativity at Work.* Harvard Business Review, 2011

American Psychological Association. "APA Dictionary of Psychology." American Psychological Association. Accessed February 5, 2026. https://dictionary.apa.org/cognitive-tunneling.

American Psychological Association. "APA Dictionary of Psychology." American Psychological Association. Accessed February 5, 2026. https://dictionary.apa.org/identity-foreclosure.

Brainz Magazine. "Breaking Through Possibility Blindness – Embracing Faith, Vision, and Transformation." Brainz Magazine, November 1, 2024. https://www.brainzmagazine.com/post/breaking-through-possibility-blindness-embracing-faith-vision-and-transformation.

"Compassion Practices." Self, January 30, 2026. https://self-compassion.org/self-compassion-practices/.

Department of Health and Human Services. "Our Epidemic of Loneliness and Isolation: The U.S. Surgeon General's Advisory on the Healing Effects of Social Connection and Community." Department of Health and Human Services, 2023. https://www.hhs.gov/sites/default/files/surgeon-general-social-connection-advisory.pdf.

Discprofile.com - disc profile. Accessed February 5, 2026. https://www.discprofile.com/.

Dunbar, Robin I.M. "The Social Brain Hypothesis†." Wiley Online Library, December 7, 1998. https://onlinelibrary.wiley.com/doi/abs/10.1002/(SICI)1520-6505(1998)6:5%3C178::AID-EVAN5%3E3.0.CO;2-8?casa_token=wflr_gB6PssAAAAA%3A-hjW_YpSrg5PLV2HsSD553ujDsTXgxdXN3T__53ktMUArX65Bnex9kxhvXCZt-UideSA31IWMd_bykDn.

Dunbar, Robin. "TEXxObserver - Robin Dunbar - Can the Internet Buy You More Friends?" TEDx Talks. YouTube, 2013. https://www.youtube.com/watch?v=07IpED729k8.

Empowering Insights. "Why Making Friends as an Adult Feels Difficult—And What to Do About It | Researcher Brené Brown." YouTube, 2025. https://www.youtube.com/watch?v=AhA_9WeXico.

Enneagram Institute, The, February 28, 2024. https://www.enneagraminstitute.com/.

Eyal, & Maytal. "Self-Silencing Is Making Women Sick." Time, October 3, 2023. https://time.com/6319549/silencing-women-sick-essay/.

Fogg, Brian J. *Tiny Habits: The Small Changes That Change Everything.* London: Virgin Books, 2020.

Forbes Council post: "How Loneliness and Remote Work Are Shaping the Employee Experience." Forbes. Accessed February 5, 2026. https://www.forbes.com/councils/forbesbusinesscouncil/2024/10/28/how-loneliness-and-remote-work-are-shaping-the-employee-experience/.

Forbes Council post: "Three Steps to Overcoming Resistance." Forbes. Accessed February 5, 2026. https://www.forbes.com/sites/forbescoachescouncil/2018/08/14/three-steps-to-overcoming-resistance/.

French Gates, Melinda. "Moments That Make Us: How Friendship Helped Oprah Winfrey & Gayle King Navigate Life's Big Changes." YouTube, 2025. https://www.youtube.com/watch?v=XBKa7PDnoVA.

Gallup, Inc. "How the CLIFTONSTRENGTHS Assessment Works." Gallup.com, September 21, 2019. https://www.gallup.com/cliftonstrengths/en/253676/how-cliftonstrengths-works.aspx.

"Gary Vaynerchuk." Wikipedia, January 17, 2026. https://en.wikipedia.org/wiki/Gary_Vaynerchuk.

Gloveworx, "Understanding Self-Efficacy to Become Unstoppable." Gloveworx. Accessed February 5, 2026. https://www.gloveworx.com/blog/understanding-self-efficacy/#:~:text=Mastery%20Experiences%20Bandura%20identified%20master%20experiences%20as,success%20is%20within%20their%20locus%20of%20control.

Harvard Graduate School of Education, "What Is Causing Our Epidemic of Loneliness and How Can We Fix It?" Harvard Graduate School of Education. Accessed February 5, 2026. https://www.gse.harvard.edu/ideas/usable-knowledge/24/10/what-causing-our-epidemic-loneliness-and-how-can-we-fix-it.

Hellman, Rick. "KU Study: Daily Chat with Friend Boosts Well-Being." KU News. Accessed February 5, 2026. https://news.ku.edu/news/article/2023/02/01/just-one-quality-conversation-friend-boosts-daily-well-being-0.

Hershfield, Hal, and Pratt, Sean. *Your Future Self: How to Make Tomorrow Better Today.* New York: Little, Brown Spark, 2023.

Holt-Lunstad, Julianne. "Social Connection as a Critical Factor for Mental and Physical Health: Evidence, Trends, Challenges, and Future Implications." World Psychiatry: Official Journal of the World Psychiatric Association (WPA), October 2024. https://pmc.ncbi.nlm.nih.gov/articles/PMC11403199/.

Itani, Omar. "The Confidence Cycle: Taking Action Is How You Boost Your Confidence." OMAR ITANI, August 23, 2021. https://www.omaritani.com/blog/boost-your-confidence.

Jack, Dana C. *Silencing the Self: Women and Depression—How to Achieve Connection in Relationships Without Losing Who You Are.* New York, New York: William Morrow Paperbacks, 1993.

Joly, Hubert, and Lambert, Caroline. *The Heart of Business: Leadership Principles for the Next Era of Capitalism.* Boston, MA: Harvard Business Review Press, 2021.

Kennedy, Dan S., and Fischer, Martin J. *No B. S. Marketing to the Affluent: No Holds Barred, Take No Prisoners, Guide to Getting Really Rich.* La Vergne: Entrepreneur Media Inc/Entrepreneur Press, 2025.

"Laurie Weingart: Collaboration, Conflict, and Negotiation Researcher." Laurie R. Weingart. Accessed February 5, 2026. https://www.laurieweingart.com/.

Lim, Annabelle G.Y. Lim Psychology Graduate BA (Hons). "Big 5 Personality Traits: The 5-Factor Model of Personality." Simply Psychology, March 20, 2025. https://www.simplypsychology.org/big-five-personality.html.

Lomibao, Niki. "The Power of Self-Advocacy: How Finding Your Voice Can Transform Your Life." Desert Blue Consulting & Coaching, September 4, 2024. https://www.desertblueaz.com/blog/the-power-of-self-advocacy-how-finding-your-voice-can-transform-your-life.

Milkman, Katherine L. *How to Change.* San Francisco, CA, USA: Kanopy Streaming, 2024.

Oprah. "Oprah and Mel Robbins Share How to Overcome Jealousy." YouTube, 2025. Oprah and Mel Robbins Share How to Overcome Jealousy.

"Oprah Winfrey." Wikipedia, January 31, 2026. https://en.wikipedia.org/wiki/Oprah_Winfrey.

Owens, Hannah, LMSW, and Morin, Amy, LCSW. "What Is Cognitive Reframing and How Does It Work?" Verywell Mind, October 17, 2025. https://www.verywellmind.com/reframing-defined-2610419.

Peetz, Johanna, Buehler, Roger, and Wells, Tayler. "Goals Out Loud: Telling Others About a Goal Increases Support Received and Facilitates Goal Pursuit." Sage Journals, October 27, 2025. https://journals.sagepub.com/doi/10.1177/01461672251382271.

Psychology Today, "Neuroplasticity." Psychology Today. Accessed February 5, 2026. https://www.psychologytoday.com/us/basics/neuroplasticity.

Psychology Today, "New Evidence That We're Wired for Connection." Psychology Today. Accessed February 5, 2026. https://www.psychologytoday.com/us/blog/best-practices-in-health/202503/new-evidence-that-were-wired-for-connection.

RevelEleven. "Science of Stuck, The: Breaking Through Inertia to Find Your Path Forward." YouTube, 2023. https://www.youtube.com/watch?v=Wjf5KC0R_LM&t=1655s.

"Sara Blakely." Wikipedia, January 31, 2026. https://en.wikipedia.org/wiki/Sara_Blakely.

Silicon Valley Historical Association. "Steve Jobs Secrets of Life." YouTube, 2012. https://www.youtube.com/watch?v=kYfNvmF0Bqw.

Sinek, Simon. *Find Your Why*. NY, NY: Portfolio/Penguin, an imprint of Penguin Random House, LLC, 2017.

Sinek, Simon. "Simon Sinek & Trevor Noah on Friendship, Loneliness, Vulnerability, and More | Full Conversation." YouTube, 2025. https://www.youtube.com/watch?v=CNBxIhxHHxM.

Staff, Newport Institute. "Why Young Women Self-Silence, and How It Impacts Mental Health." Newport Institute, January 13, 2026. https://www.newportinstitute.com/resources/empowering-young-adults/self-silencing/#:~:text=Key%20Takeaways,their%20partner%20and%20the%20world.

"Steve Jobs." Wikipedia, February 4, 2026. https://en.wikipedia.org/wiki/Steve_Jobs.

Stieg, Cory. "How to Stay Committed to Your Goals: Tell Someone More Successful than You, Says New Study." CNBC, September 5, 2019. https://www.cnbc.com/2019/09/05/why-sharing-goals-with-someone-helps-you-achieve-them.html.

TEDx Talks. "Secret to Self-Advocacy, The | Bhavana Bartholf | TEDxWaterStreet." YouTube, 2023. https://www.youtube.com/watch?v=FkgQ9f7KJaw.

Trevor-Roberts. "How to Avoid the Negative Impacts of a Career Plateau." Trevor, August 1, 2024. https://blog.trevor-roberts.com.au/how-to-avoid-the-negative-impacts-of-a-career-plateau.

Weingart, Laurie. "Collaboration and Conflict in Teams - Laurie Weingart." YouTube, 2021. https://www.youtube.com/watch?v=Xqk5zvjln-E.

Wiley Online Library, "Feeling Stuck and Feeling Bad: Career Plateaus, Negative Emotions, and Counterproductive Work Behaviors - ng - 2024 - Human Resource Management Journal." Wiley Online Library. Accessed February 5, 2026. https://onlinelibrary.wiley.com/doi/10.1111/1748-8583.12539.

Wood, Jenny. *Wild Courage: Go After What You Want and Get It.* New York: Portfolio/Penguin, 2025.

"You Have More Influence than You Think - Vanessa K. Bohns." Vanessa Bohns. Accessed February 5, 2026. https://www.vanessabohns.com/book/you-have-more-influence-than-you-think.

About the Author

Candice Mitchell is the CEO of The Talent Collective, the company behind the Talent Development Academy®, a global ecosystem designed to build strategic, confident People teams that drive real business results.

With a *Master of Science in Organizational Leadership with a concentration in Strategic Innovation and Change* and nearly two decades leading Learning, Talent, and Change strategies across industries, Candice has helped organizations transform their people functions from "support" to business-critical growth drivers.

Known for her energy, straight-talking style, and deep expertise, she partners with People teams to connect capability to performance and create lasting impact through workshops, tools, and frameworks used by companies worldwide.

Her perspective is deeply shaped by how she grew up. Candice's parents were serial entrepreneurs armed with a Grade 10, a Grade 12, endless creativity, and sheer determination. Watching them build, adapt, and back themselves taught her early lessons about capability, resilience, and what's possible when people are trusted to figure things out.

Candice married her husband Darryl in 2014, welcomed their son in 2015 and their daughter in 2017, and shares life with a very high-maintenance Weimaraner named Shackleton, best described as regal and entirely aware of it.

Originally from South Africa, the family moved to the United States in 2019 to chase bigger dreams and now lives in the foothills of the Rocky Mountains. Adventurous by nature, they're happiest exploring new places together, whether that's across oceans or up mountain roads. They ski together proudly, even though Candice was almost 40 the first time she ever saw snow and remains firmly a baby-blue skier.